Preface

This report has been produced at a time when far-reaching economic, political, social and ideological changes have been taking place in Europe. In the course of discussions between ministers on the 'harmonization' of policies, many states have adopted increasingly restrictive measures on asylum. Across Europe measures have been introduced which prevent asylum-seekers reaching European states to make a claim for asylum; and which reduce the proportion of asylum-seekers granted protection. Little consideration has been given to the possibility that changes in Europe could have an impact in the treatment of refugees across the world; yet the logical consequence of these restrictions is a ripple effect which could exclude refugees from wider and wider areas. Ultimately this could lead to a fundamental crisis of the whole institution of asylum; a crisis leading to the downgrading of protection for refugees. This is set against a background of unprecedented levels of (frequently unsympathetic) coverage in the media.

Prior to 1989 refugees had attracted scant media attention, and the coverage that was given dwelt on refugees as victims of torture or as defenders of democracy and human rights. More recently refugees and asylum-seekers have been portrayed in the media and in public debate as 'burdensome', a 'threat', or even as 'criminals'. Many characteristics formerly attributed to immigrants to Europe are now attributed to refugees. Many of the themes of ethnicity, belonging, nationality and xenophobia are now being increasingly debated in the arena of refugees, rather than in relation to immigrants. With immigration channels largely closed, refugees have become the new target.

It is commonly believed that Europe attracts a higher proportion of asylum-seekers than other parts of the world. This report documents evidence that most refugees are to be found in countries of the South with many African, Asian and Middle Eastern states accommodating a far higher number of refugees in relation to their overall population than any country in Europe. European ministers have also argued that refugees should flee to countries neighbouring or close to their own, and yet when an exodus of peoples fleeing 'ethnic cleansing' in the former Yugoslavia occurred, many European nations imposed visa restrictions to prevent these asylum-seekers reaching their shores.

It is difficult to predict for how long countries in Africa, Asia and the Middle East will continue to host large refugee populations without seeking to follow the example of European states and impose similarly restrictive measures. Because most cannot control their borders in the same way, there is a threat that refugees will be expelled. Soon there may be nowhere for a would-be refugee to turn. Not only will this serve to undermine a long tradition of shelter for those who were unable to seek protection from their own governments, but it will impact on the willingness and ability of communities and individuals to resist and survive persecution, torture and gross abuses of human rights. It will take the world a step backwards in its knowledge of, and ability to address, human rights and minority rights abuses across the world.

This Report is an updated and revised edition of the Report *Refugees in Europe*, which was published in 1990. This new edition includes a wealth of information on the legislative changes and brings a fresh focus on the situation facing those fleeing from war in the former Yugoslavia. In addition the report analyzes the move towards a common, far tougher European approach to asylum-seekers which inevitably results in the closing of the doors to many refugees.

This Report is intended to contribute to a better understanding of the complex refugee issue in Europe. It aims to provide a clear explanation of the current refugee situation, give the facts and point out the issues which need to be addressed. The main author of this report, Dr Danièle Joly, is a French academic based at the Centre for Research in Ethnic Relations at the University of Warwick in the UK. She has written widely on the subject and has for many years specialized in detailed studies of refugees in Europe, including case studies of particular refugee groups and analysis of policy issues. Lynette Kelly has provided much of the statistical information, created the graphs, and assisted with new material for this Report.

The authors show that changes made in individual European countries, have often derived from agreements reached at meetings between ministers. These meetings have not been held under the auspices of the European Union and are not subject to democratic scrutiny or control. However, they are commonly perceived as being part of a wider European package and seem difficult to challenge because of this. If the situation of refugees in Europe (and throughout the world) is not to deteriorate further, politicians should understand that decisions made in this way have a very limited legitimacy and will be challenged.

Alan Phillips
Director
February 1997

Introduction

Refugees are always a minority in their countries of asylum. Refugees are often a minority in their country of origin, persecuted by a repressive regime on the grounds of their ethnic group, religion, language or their political beliefs. Yet refugees are not negligible in numbers. Worldwide the United Nations High Commissioner for Refugees (UNHCR) recognizes over 15 million refugees and asylum-seekers in need of international protection and/or assistance, in addition to millions of 'internally displaced peoples'. However only a small proportion of the total population of Western Europe are refugees. Yet, in general, refugees in Europe are unwelcome arrivals for governments, and their accounts of torture and persecution are often disbelieved. Those who are accepted for asylum, however, are frequently abused, ignored or patronized.

All too often, media images and ministerial statements present the movement of refugees into European countries as something new and threatening. But the reality is different; Europe has both created and received refugees for centuries. The continent was the source of modern mass movements and of the development of the international system to provide protection and assistance. Current refugee movements, and the crisis in refugee protection, are part of a long-term historical process. As modern nation-states have established themselves and European empires have risen and collapsed, refugees have been part of the landscape as victims of struggles for control and dominance. Earlier refugees fled religious persecution; approximately 200,000 French Huguenots to the Low Countries, England, Germany and Switzerland between 1681 and 1685, and Jews from the Russian Empire fled westwards in the nineteenth and early twentieth centuries. The First World War and its aftermath saw the growth of the modern refugee movement. Vast numbers of people were forced from their homes in the face of war on an unprecedented scale, and the nationalist struggles which emerged from the ending of the Russian, Austro-Hungarian and Ottoman Empires left isolated national minorities in the states of Central and Southern Europe.

In the 1930s Spanish Republicans, pursued by Franco's army, sought refuge in France and other European countries, together with the Jews, Roma (Gypsies) political activists and others who fell victim to Hitler's fascism. Even then European governments were often less than generous in their treatment of Jewish asylum-seekers. The immediate post-Second World War period saw Europe full of refugees directly resulting from the war or from the Cold War which followed; over 6 million people are estimated to have been displaced within Europe. Some refugees left the continent, scattering across a world searching for additional workers to support their economic recovery. In 1956 many refugees fled from Hungary and again in 1968 from the former Czechoslovakia following the brutal repression of the national uprising. These refugees escaped to many parts of Europe and over several decades have, in general, settled successfully.

The Report shows how more recently, the pattern of refugee movements has changed. As new independent states have emerged from colonial rule, the main refugee movements have originated from these areas – Africa, Asia, the Middle East – and also from repressive regimes in Latin America. More recently still, thousands have fled from the civil war in former Yugoslavia. By far the greatest number remained in the regions from which they came, however, the number of asylum-seekers in Europe has increased in the last decade (see below). In the 1960s, for example, whatever other problems refugees might have faced, most could have found employment, however menial. But at a time of serious economic recession, unemployment and a rebuttal to immigrants, this new wave of refugees has not been welcomed by most European governments.

A feature of the Report is its detailed exploration not only of the civil and political rights of asylum-seekers but also their economic, social and cultural rights. There is little value in being offered asylum if it is amid appalling conditions, where no employment is available, where refugees suffer racial abuse and are dependent on welfare aid from others. The complexity of the subject even for dealing with one group in one country at one period of time, is worthy of a report on its own; hence the Report is an overview with many references to enable the interested reader to explore a specific topic in depth.

Mass movements

Although mass exoduses have existed since ancient times, it is only in the twentieth century that refugee movements have become an international political issue requiring international legal instruments and political agreements as the framework for their solution.

There have been attempts to document and analyze the causes of modern refugee movements. Marrus[1] noted three distinguishing factors. First, there was the dramatic rise in refugee numbers. Second, the movements were accompanied by a radically new form of homelessness. As nation-states took over the civil functions formerly provided by the church and local communities, refugees became increasingly marginalized:

> 'Outside the state from which they had come, refugees could not work, could not live, could not live unmolested, could usually not remain at liberty for any length of time ... modern refugees ... differed from those of earlier times because their homelessness removed them so dramatically and uniquely from civil society'.

An earlier scholar, Hope-Simpson, remarked in 1939 that:

> 'The whole system [of nationality] is based on a scheme of national states, with populations which fit into the scheme of nationalities. The person without a nationality, and without the protection of their national representatives does not fit into that system'.[2]

Third, Marrus noted that the duration of exile increased and refugee camps became common as attempts were made to find solutions to the problems this growing class of uprooted people presented their often reluctant hosts.[3]

The First World War and the dissolution of the 'old Europe'

If it was the formation of the new nation-states that made life so difficult for refugees, it was the dissolution of the old Europe and the bloody birth of the modern era that lay at the root of the growing crisis. The number of people displaced across international boundaries in the four years of the First World War equalled the numbers who moved in the 20 years following it. After the war, many of those who had moved – Belgians, Lithuanians, Poles, Serbs, Russians – returned to their homes.[4] But there were large numbers who did not, and many refugees were rendered stateless as new nations and new borders were established. Jewish refugees, in particular, found themselves without a state which would claim them.[5]

As the old order collapsed, refugee numbers grew rapidly. Mechanisms to deal with their plight became more urgent. In the Balkans, the First World War finally completed the long disintegration of the Ottoman Empire. With its multiplicity of ethnic, linguistic and religious groups – all seeking to establish their claim to a national territory – conflicts were extremely violent and refugees fled ever more horrific massacres. Armenians, Assyrians, Chaldeans, Jews, Macedonians, Serbs and Turks fled from the advances of each other's armies.[6]

Birth of an international refugee system

It was the 1917 Russian Revolution and its aftermath that led to the establishment of an international system for refugee questions. More than a million refugees fled over the changing Soviet borders between 1917 and 1921.[7] While non-governmental organizations (NGOs) had provided assistance and relief to refugees, these were not sufficient to address the problems. Governments 'had to find ways of working together to address refugee and displaced persons problems that outstripped the capacity of individual states'.[8]

In 1921 Fridjof Nansen was appointed by the League of Nations as 'High Commissioner on Behalf of the League in connection with the Problem of Russian Refugees in Europe'. A famous Norwegian explorer, Nansen had been involved in a private capacity in negotiating the repatriation of Russian and Austro-Hungarian prisoners of war.[9] His appointment marked the emergence of the first formal attempt to establish an international system to deal with refugee issues. Support, however, was tentative: Nansen was given only administrative support by the League; NGOs provided the staff and supplies.

Nansen's preferred option was to seek the repatriation of refugees, but he was clear that this should be voluntary. He therefore established a principle which was to become central to refugee law and practice.[10] Many refugees, however, did not want to return, and both they and the political opponents of the new Soviet regime ensured that refugees were allowed either to remain in the countries to which they had fled or were resettled elsewhere.

Because nationality had become increasingly important, documentation was required to enable refugees to move on. Many of the refugees were stateless and a travel document, the 'Nansen passport' was awarded to specific national groups who had lost the protection of their state of origin: to Russian refugees (in 1922), Armenians (in 1924), Assyrians, Assyro-Chaldeans, Kurds, Syrians and Turks (all in 1928).

The Second World War and its aftermath

Events leading up to, during, and immediately following the Second World War, heralded a radical rethinking of the international structures for dealing with refugees. In the 1930s specific national groups, including refugees from Germany (1936 and 1938) and Sudeten refugees from the former Czechoslovakia (1939) were able to benefit from international conventions and resolutions.[11] However, 'the real story and tragedy of this period is not those refugees that fled their countries and were not helped, but those that remained behind for a variety of reasons.'[12] These included the individual Russians and other Soviet citizens unable to escape Stalin's purges of the 1930s, and, most dramatically, the victims of the Holocaust.

Although the League of Nations had established a 'High Commission for Refugees (Jewish and other) coming from Germany' in 1933, it had been unable to provide protection for those who were trying to escape. The first High Commissioner, James G. McDonald resigned in December 1935 in protest at his inability to deal effectively with the situation.[13] In his letter of resignation McDonald argued that it was not sufficient to attempt to alleviate the circumstances of people who had fled; political action was required to address the causes.[14] Jews seeking to leave Germany were prevented from doing so because they had to sacrifice their financial assets. At a time of economic depression they were unable to fulfil the condition of potential host countries that they should not become a burden to the public purse.

The Evian Conference called by President Roosevelt in mid-1938 failed because of the refusal of Germany to allow Jews to leave with their assets, and the refusal of potential resettlement countries to accept any financial burden. The UK blocked the possibility of resettlement in Palestine which it administered under a League of Nations mandate. The conference established the Intergovernmental Committee on Refugees which was mandated, but failed, to negotiate an orderly process of migration.[15]

In the face of the international community's failure to provide a solution, increasing numbers of Jews fled Germany despite the dangers and the lack of certainty on the other side of the border. By the outbreak of war in 1939 there were an estimated 100,000, mainly Jewish, refugees in Europe who had not been resettled.[16]

As the war progressed, the number of refugees and displaced people rose to an unprecedented level. One estimate[17] is that 60 million civilians were forced to move from their homes. Many thousands of refugees did manage to escape, but it was the Holocaust that convinced the international community, and particularly the European and North American governments, of the urgent need to find a way forward.

In the immediate aftermath of the war the Allies were faced with the immense task of finding a secure home for millions of displaced people and refugees. The United Nations Relief and Rehabilitation Agency (UNRRA) was set up to enable them to be resettled. Its task was made even more complicated by the expulsion of over 12 million ethnic Germans from the areas of today's Central and Eastern Europe which was occupied by Soviet forces.[18] By 1947 when UNRRA was replaced by the International Refugee Organization (IRO) there were still over 1 million refugees in Europe.[19]

Working outside the UN system, IRO focused primarily on resettlement. With the post-war economic recovery demanding more workers, the organization was highly successful in its task. But as the years passed, new crises, particularly in Central and Eastern Europe indicated that refugees were not going to disappear. In December 1950, as the IRO mandate expired, the Office of the United Nations High Commissioner for Refugees (UNHCR) was established, with the first High Commissioner taking office on 1 January 1951. On 28 July 1951, an important refugee convention – the Geneva Convention – came into operation.

Conventions and categories

As the major international institution dealing with refugees, UNHCR's main role is to protect refugees, and to encourage governments to accept and take care of them. UNHCR is a major intergovernmental body upholding the Mandate and Convention relating to the status of refugees and has been financed by governments. Its responsibilities also entail giving information, advising decision-making authorities and, more rarely, taking part in the determination of refugee status. In some countries it provides or finances legal advice for asylum-seekers. In theory, UNHCR is an independent and humanitarian non-political organization. However, its position is delicate as it is financed by states which might try to exert influence to reflect their specific government policies,[20] and there are representatives of countries which have produced refugees on its Executive Committee.

The 1951 Geneva Convention

With the failure of the League of Nations system to protect individuals because of its emphasis on national groups, the 1951 UN Convention on the Status of Refugees attempted to provide a universal definition. Under the Convention a person cannot claim refugee status on the grounds of membership of a particular national group as had been the case up until the Second World War, but must justify individual persecution on specific grounds. This has been portrayed as a shift to the recognition and protection of individual **'human rights' refugees** rather than the collective recognition of **'humanitarian' refugees**.[21]

The 1951 Convention defines a refugee as any person who:

> 'As a result of events occurring before 1 January 1951 and owing to well-founded fear of being persecuted for reasons of race, religion, nationality, membership of a particular social group or political opinion, is outside the country of his [sic] nationality and is unable to or, owing to such fear, is unwilling to avail himself of the protection of that country and return to it.'

In addition to the limitation on time, the Convention also allowed states to decide whether the events referred to relate to events 'occurring in Europe' or 'in Europe or elsewhere'. Most states signing the Convention initially confined the definition to events in Europe.

With its restrictions of time and geography the Convention was intended to address the problems created by the post-Second World War turmoils and the Cold War. The High Commissioner's mandate was originally set for three years; it was thought that the refugee crisis facing Europe could be dealt with in a relatively short time. Unfortunately this has not proved to be the case, and the 1951 Convention remains the major international instrument in the field of refugee law. In 1967, the Bellagio Protocol extended the provisions of the Convention to post-1951 events.

Interpreting the Convention and evaluating claims

The Convention's definition lends itself to a variety of interpretations. Its central clause incorporates objective and subjective criteria: not only persecution, but fear of persecution. 'Persecution' is difficult enough to define precisely, but 'fear', even if it has to be 'well-founded', is far more elusive. Although UNHCR has produced a detailed *Handbook on Procedures and Criteria for Determining Refugee Status*,[22] interpretation of the criteria depends on the approach of government officials who make the decisions in line with current state policies. Such evaluation has changed over time,[23] for example, many of the Europeans for whom the definition was designed might not have been granted refugee status if the Convention had been applied in the same way as it is today.[24] This reflects shifting attitudes in Western Europe, and a radical change in attitudes to immigration following the post-war recovery period which allowed for the easy absorption of the Hungarians, and the subsequent economic collapse of the 1970s which led to the restrictions on immigration into Western Europe, particularly on people from 'developing' countries. A generally hostile attitude to refugees replaced the previously favourable attitudes.

The Convention stipulates states' obligations to refugees who are granted refugee status. Most important is the prohibition of *refoulement*: states are prohibited from expelling or returning a refugee to a country where he or she risks persecution. Other clauses detail obligations concerning the delivery of identity documents, employment, education, and welfare. Apart from the non-*refoulement* clause, these provisions offer states a large measure of flexibility which can range from treatment on a par with nationals to the more limited rights and entitlements accorded to other foreigners.

As of 1995, 127 states are signatory to the 1951 Convention and the 1967 Protocol.[25] In principle, states which grant the status of refugee are not bound to grant territorial asylum, but in practice European states have done so. All 23 members of the Council of Europe[26] have signed the 1951 Convention, and only Hungary and Turkey have limited Convention status to Europeans.

Decolonization, underdevelopment and 'new refugees'

The 1967 Protocol reflected historical developments in 'developing' countries resulting from a combination of causes including decolonization, the formation of new states, underdevelopment, class and ethnic conflicts, and superpower rivalries – together these have been the root causes which have led to civil wars, revolutions and dictatorships. Improved and cheaper transport, particularly by air, has made it possible for a growing number of refugees from 'developing' countries to seek asylum in Europe. As they began to arrive in the 1970s they were called 'new refugees', distinguishing them from their European predecessors.[27]

However, the 1951 Convention excludes some people who need protection: for example, victims of generalized violence. In a number of cases such people are protected by UNHCR through a procedure known as 'good offices'. First used in 1957 this procedure was extended by a resolution of the UN General Assembly in 1959 to include all groups of refugees 'who do not come within the competence of the United Nations'.[28] Many of the large groups of refugees in 'developing' countries have benefited from this procedure over the past two decades.

'Developing' country initiatives

With so many refugees originating in 'developing' countries, it is from there that new advances have been made in the legal provisions for refugees. In 1969 the Organization of African Unity (OAU) Convention was adopted which broadens the definition of refugees to include:[29]

> 'Every person who, owing to external aggression, occupation, foreign domination or events seriously disturbing public order in either part or the whole of his [sic] country of origin or nationality, is compelled to leave his place of habitual residence in order to seek refuge in another place outside his country of origin or nationality.'

Most refugees qualifying under this definition have been resettled in countries neighbouring their homeland, particularly in Africa. But increasing numbers have been arriving in Europe in the 1980s and 1990s. The Cartagena Declaration of 1984[30] which was adopted by the Organization of American States (OAS) in 1985 also contains a broader definition, including:

> 'Persons who have fled their country because their lives, safety or freedom have been threatened by generalized violence, foreign aggression, internal conflicts, massive violation of human rights or other circumstances which have seriously disturbed the public order.'

Other regional international conventions on asylum concern the Americas but they do not add to the definitions presented above; the 1928 Havana Convention on Asylum, the 1933 Montevideo Convention on Political Asylum, and the 1954 Caracas Conventions on Territorial Asylum and Diplomatic Asylum.

Other groups

Two other categories, not explicitly included in the 1951 Convention, have been given specific consideration: women and conscientious objectors to military service. The Executive Committee of the UNHCR programme indicated in 1985 that states were free to grant refugee status to women on the grounds that they were persecuted as a 'particular social group' within the terms of the 1951 Convention. Furthermore, according to a Resolution adopted at the Council of Ministers in Copenhagen on 1 June 1993, women who have been subjected to severe sexual assault who have no assistance near their home are included in 'vulnerable groups', and may be offered temporary protection.

Until the early 1990s, Sweden allowed deserters and war resisters to seek protection. The UN Commission on Human Rights recognized conscientious objection as a valid expression of human rights which has made it possible in some cases (Canada, USA) to establish a claim for asylum based on military desertion.

Other international and European instruments exist which enable states to offer protection, for example: the 1984 UN Convention against Torture and Other Cruel, Inhuman or Degrading Treatment or Punishment (which has been signed by France among others), and the 1950 Council of Europe Convention for the Protection of Human Rights and Fundamental Freedoms. It has also been argued that the determination of refugee status ought to be based on the violations of the standards of the UN Universal Declaration of Human Rights[31] which stipulates that: 'Everyone has the right to seek and to enjoy in other countries asylum from persecution' (Article 14 [1]).

An emerging ethic of human rights

No absolute definition or international law on refugees exists, nor is it practicable. Taken together, the conventions and resolutions represent an internationally-accepted ethic of human rights which has emerged in response to changing circumstances.[32] But the right to asylum is limited even under these conventions. Refugees are guaranteed the right to 'seek' asylum but not to obtain it: it is the sole prerogative of the state to recognize refugees and grant them asylum on its territory.[33] This prerogative has become increasingly emphasized in recent years.

Categories and statuses

The scope for interpretation offered by the Convention has resulted in widely different applications in Europe. Several legal and social categories of 'refugees' have emerged which vary from country to country and whose rights also vary.

Convention refugees are granted refugee status under the 1951 Geneva Convention. They are divided into two groups. First, there are 'quota' refugees who are taken in as a group and/or under a programme, such as the Vietnamese in several European countries (quotas may include mixed nationalities while only one nationality comes under the programme). Second, there are 'spontaneous' refugees who arrive in Europe on their own accord and make an application for asylum according to a national procedure. (People applying for refugee status are known as **asylum-seekers** while they are awaiting a decision.)

Because Italy ratified the Convention and Protocol with a geographical limitation excluding non-Europeans, it was the only European country with **Mandate refugees** recognized under the UNHCR mandate. New legislation in 1990 removed the limitation. In other Western European countries there is generally no distinction between Convention and Mandate refugees.

If asylum-seekers are not recognized they are not necessarily expelled. So-called **humanitarian status** or *de facto* **refugees** are allowed to stay in the country for humanitarian reasons under another status than that of the Convention: status B or C in Scandinavian countries; *asilo* in Spain; exceptional leave to remain in the UK; *assimilé à refugié* in Belgium; *duldung* in Germany.[34] The variety in status in different countries arises from *ad hoc* legal responses of states to changes in the nature of refugee movements, and an unwillingness of European states to recognize many asylum-seekers under the Convention. The rights enjoyed under such status are generally much more limited than those of Convention refugees; this has caused a debate on their legitimacy. Many NGOs argue that *de facto* status is being used as a means of enabling refugees to be settled without the rights and in worse conditions than if they were granted refugee status. In the UK, for example, **refugees with exceptional leave to remain** are not allowed to be joined by their families for four years, while those with Convention status have an immediate right of family reunion.

The Council of Europe has expressed its concern about the situation of *de facto* refugees'.[35] While acknowledging that such people fall outside the scope of the 1951 Convention, there were valid reasons for people being unable to return. These would include a reasonable belief that they would be unable to exercise their human rights, be discriminated against or be compelled to act in a manner incompatible with their conscience. In addition, war or serious public disorder are advanced as valid reasons for refusal to return. **Refugees in orbit** refers to a phenomenon where refugees are sent from country to country, with no country willing to accept responsibility and examine their request for asylum.

UNHCR has denounced 'legalistic and static' approaches. People should be given some form of asylum and humane treatment if they have valid reasons for not wanting to return home even if they do not qualify in terms of the Convention.[36]

With the mass movement of refugees resulting from the war in former Yugoslavia, a new category, the notion of '**temporary protection**' – with the sole prospect of their return as soon as the situation permits – has been introduced.

Who is a refugee?

Given the variety of definitions and legal categories, what characterizes refugees and differentiates them from other migrants? One essential feature is that refugees are involuntary migrants: in short, they did not want to leave:

> 'With a different goal and with motivations at variance with those affecting voluntary migrants, the refugee moves from his [sic] homeland to the country of his settlement against his will. He is a distinct social type ... It is the reluctance to uproot oneself, and the absence of positive original motivations to settle elsewhere, which characterizes all refugee decisions and distinguishes the refugee from the voluntary migrants.'[37]

Kunz argues that this applies whether people are '**anticipatory**' **refugees**, who foresee the crisis, or '**emergency**' **refugees**, who are victims of it. Zolberg develops a more detailed analysis from a study of refugee movements worldwide, and identifies three main types: dissenters, target groups and bystanders. They share one characteristic that merges the three categories into a coherent set and distinguishes them from others: violence.[38] Violence encompasses a range of situations including indirectly-inflicted violence, 'by way of imposed conditions that make normal life impossible'. Furthermore, Hathaway argues that disenfranchisement from one's home society in a fundamental manner, is a common element to all refugee situations.[39]

The involuntary character of refugees' departure is not always easy to identify. For example, loss of one's livelihood can result from economic causes such as a recession, but particular groups or individuals may suffer especially because they are deprived of land, employment or education as a result of political persecution. Natural disasters can also have discriminatory political consequences, and also, in any case compel people to flee.

New realities and the need for new definitions

The realities of the modern refugee phenomenon might justify a re-evaluation of issues and definitions. Legal definitions and international conventions have evolved to include and exclude various groups and individuals on different criteria according to the character of a particular period.[40]

The 1951 Convention definition with its provisions for recognition on the basis of individual persecution was a response to the horrors of the Holocaust and the realignment of Europe following the Second World War. It changed the status of refugees recognized under previous agreements with the result that there were several categories of refugee, each with a different official status. For two decades the 1951 Convention, complemented by the 1967 Protocol, seemed to satisfy the needs of refugees. The definition was interpreted liberally, and immigration policies were relaxed.

But from the early 1970s, the strict immigration policies of most European states have added new elements to the question of asylum. Governments and parts of the media have tended to portray asylum-seekers as immigrants in disguise. They fail to note that many immigrants of the 1960s and 1970s were refugees 'in disguise'. Liberal immigration policies allowed entry without their having to claim refugee status, an easier route taken by, for example, many Kurdish and Turkish refugees going to Germany. There are further complications where the same circumstances give rise to both refugees and economic immigrants. Economic depression causes economic migration, but it can also create unrest resulting in repression and refugee movements.

Although it is not always easy to make clear distinctions between refugees and immigrants, it is essential to do so, as their situation is covered by different national and international legislation and conventions. Closing the borders to non-European (EU) immigrants while increasing the pace of European integration has led to a stricter and more limited interpretation of the 1951 Convention precisely at a time when refugee needs have become greater.

A major debate centres on the issue of whether the 1951 Convention is adequate, or whether it should be revised or complemented by European agreements incorporating criteria to be found in the UN Universal Declaration of Human Rights, the UN Convention on Torture, the OAU Convention, the Cartagena Declaration and the Council of Europe recommendations and resolutions. Opponents of any change, particularly NGOs, consistently argued that the 1951 Geneva definition could accommodate all refugees if it was liberally interpreted. In addition, they feared that, given present trends, European states would take advantage of any opportunity to introduce measures which would be even more restrictive. In 1993, however, the European Council on Refugees and Exiles (ECRE) stressed the need for a supplementary refugee definition.[41] As we turn to an examination of the number and origins of refugees in Europe, another major question remains: how far will the recently-adopted temporary protection formula be used in the future?

Arrivals and recognition

Statistics on asylum-seekers and refugees in Europe need to be treated with caution. Detailed information is often difficult to obtain and where data is available, great care needs to be taken when trying to make comparisons between countries or in drawing conclusions. The information available for each country varies in the definitions used and amount of detail included. When referring to the number of claims for asylum in a particular year, some countries will include arrivals under UN quotas or special temporary protection measures while others will exclude these from the total. Some countries count the number of cases, while others count the number of individuals involved in asylum applications. There are differences between the way countries define asylum-seekers; and while one country can give statistics which include every request for asylum, another country might exclude from its records all those who are turned away at the border. While one country might be able to give a full analysis of the nationality of asylum-seekers, another may not collect this type of information. Although there have been inter-government discussions and agreements on asylum-seekers and refugees within the EU, every country has its own legislation and way of processing and deciding on asylum claims, and its own way of assembling data.

In spite of the limitations imposed by the reliability and availability of data, it is possible to discern trends in the situation of asylum-seekers and refugees in Europe. Throughout this section, wherever reference is made to 'Europe', a listing of the country data used will be given in an endnote. However, in general, 'Europe' will mean the countries of Western Europe.

UNHCR has estimated that the world total of refugees and asylum-seekers in need of international protection and/or assistance stood at 15,337,000 at the end of 1995.[42] Of these, 5.2 million were in Africa; 5.5 million were in the Middle East; 1.4 million were in South and Central Asia; 453,000 were in East Asia and the Pacific; 256,000 were in the Americas; and 2.5 million were in Europe, including Central and Eastern Europe. The vast majority of the refugees and asylum-seekers in Europe are to be found in the countries of the former Soviet Union and the former Yugoslavia.

The total number of people of concern to UNHCR rose from 17 million in 1991 to more than 26 million in 1996. This includes approximately 13.2 million refugees, 3.3 million returnees, as well as 4.7 million internally displaced. Taken together with an estimated number of at least 30 million internally displaced persons worldwide, the total number of people who have been forced to flee their homes amounts to almost 50 million.[43]

Asylum applications

Figure 1 shows the number of asylum applications in Europe[44] between 1983 and 1995, compared to the number of awards of Convention refugee status. After several years when the number of asylum applications increased annually, the trend in applications now seems to be falling. The number of applications for asylum in Europe rose almost every year from 1983, when there were 73,700 applications, reaching a peak of 692,685 in 1992, but the number of applications has decreased every year since then and in 1995 there were 283,416 applications. The number of people awarded full refugee status under the UN Convention was 19,868 in 1983, this figure peaked at 46,767 in 1993, and subsequently fell slightly to 43,100 in 1995.

The number of applications for asylum in selected European countries during the same period are shown in **Figures 2.1, 2.2,** and **2.3**. These indicate the variation between countries in the annual number of asylum applications. In Belgium, Denmark and Spain, the number of applications for asylum increased between 1988 and 1993, but there was a decline in applications in 1994 and 1995. Asylum applications in the Netherlands followed a similar pattern, except the number of applications reached its peak a year later, in 1994, and then fell in 1995. In Germany applications for asylum increased every year between 1987 and 1992; and the numbers reduced in the following years. Applications for asylum in France have declined every year since 1989. The pattern of applications in the UK is somewhat different although the number of applications reached a peak in 1991 and declined in the following two years; in 1994 and 1995 an increase in the number of asylum-seekers was recorded. Provisional figures for 1996[45] however, suggest, that the total number of applications in 1996 will be less than that in 1995.

Figures 3.1, 3.2, and **3.3** show the distribution of asylum applications between the countries of Europe[46] in 1985, 1990, and 1995 respectively. In each year over 40 per cent of Europe's asylum-seekers were in Germany. In 1985 the countries with the largest share of asylum seekers were Germany (45 per cent), France (15 per cent), and Sweden (9 per cent). By 1995, although Germany is still by far the major recipient of applications for asylum, the pattern of distribution among the other European countries has changed, and the countries with the most applications are now Germany (46 per cent), UK (16 per cent) and the Netherlands (11 per cent).

As well as being distributed unevenly in absolute numerical terms, asylum-seekers are also distributed unevenly in relation to population size. **Table 1** shows the ratio of asylum-seekers to total population in selected countries in 1995. From this table it can be seen that Germany had a ratio of 633 residents to every asylum-

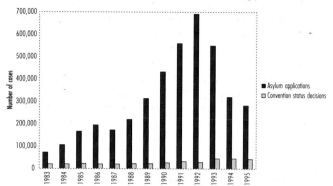

Figure 1: Asylum applications and Convention status decisions in Europe, 1983–95

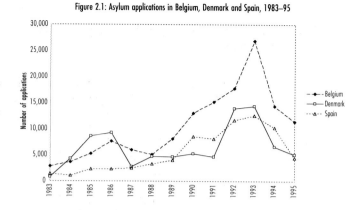

Figure 2.1: Asylum applications in Belgium, Denmark and Spain, 1983–95

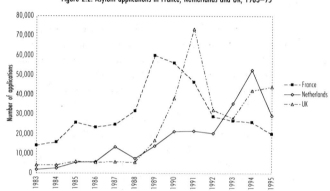

Figure 2.2: Asylum applications in France, Netherlands and UK, 1983–95

Figure 2.3: Asylum applications in Germany, 1983–95

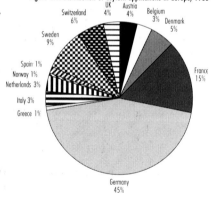

Figure 3.1: Distribution of asylum applications in Europe, 1985

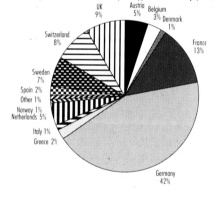

Figure 3.2: Distribution of asylum applications in Europe, 1990

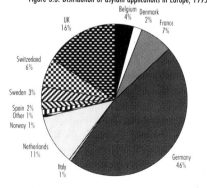

Figure 3.3: Distribution of asylum applications in Europe, 1995

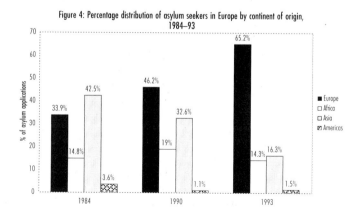

Figure 4: Percentage distribution of asylum seekers in Europe by continent of origin, 1984–93

Table 1: Asylum-seekers compared to total population in selected countries, 1995

	Population (millions)	Asylum seekers/ refugees	Ratio Asylum seekers to population
Belgium	9.9	11,409	1:872
Denmark	5.2	5,112	1:1007
France	58.0	20,170	1:2876
Germany	81.0	127,937	1:633
Italy	57.6	1,732	1:33300
Netherlands	14.9	29,258	1:509
Norway	4.3	1,460	1:2945
Spain	39.0	4,429	1:8806
Sweden	8.8	9,046	1:972
UK	58.4	17,021	1:3431
Croatia	4.5	189,500	1:24
Iran	61.3	2,075,500	1:29
Jordan	4.1	1,294,800	1:3
Lebanon	3.7	348,300	1:11
Syria	14.7	342,000	1:43
Uganda	21.3	230,000	1:93

N.B. Figures for Jordan, Lebanon, Croatia, Iran, Syria and Uganda are for refugees

Source: *World Refugee Survey*

seeker. The Netherlands, which had the third highest number of applications, actually had the smallest ratio, with 509 residents to every asylum-seeker. The UK, which had the second highest number of applications for asylum, had a much larger ratio, and came after, Belgium, Denmark, France, Norway and Sweden when population size was taken into account.

Countries of origin

Recently there has been an increase in the proportion of asylum-seekers originating from Europe, and a decrease in the proportion originating from Africa. **Figure 4** shows the percentage of asylum-seekers in Europe from each continent in 1984, 1990 and 1993.[47] In 1984, 42.5 per cent of all asylum-seekers originated from Asia and 33.9 per cent originated from Europe. By 1993 the pattern had changed markedly, and applications from European nationals made up 65.2 per cent of all asylum applications made in Europe. This results from the conflict which accompanied the disintegration of the Soviet Union and of Yugoslavia. In contrast the proportion of asylum-seekers coming from Asian countries fell to 16.3 per cent (this is due largely to the decrease in arrivals from Vietnam). **Figure 4.1** shows the percentage distribution

of asylum applications by continent of origin in selected European countries. This illustrates the wide variations between countries. Most of the asylum-seekers in Germany are from Europe. Europeans also form the largest proportion of asylum-seekers in Belgium, Denmark, France, the Netherlands and the UK, but in Spain the largest proportion of asylum-seekers is from the Americas. The country of origin of asylum-seekers in selected countries is given in **Table 2**, which lists the five largest groups by nationality in 1992 and 1995.

Temporary protection and refugees from former Yugoslavia

A major new development in the 1990s has been the existence of temporarily protected people in Europe, fleeing from the war in former Yugoslavia. The conflict in former Yugoslavia led to the displacement of many thousands of people. In July 1992 the UNHCR called for a response which was comprehensive and humanitarian, while also recognizing the temporary and emergency nature of the need for assistance.[48] UNHCR felt that because of the large numbers of people involved it would not be possible for each claim for asylum to be individually assessed, and so some form of response other than consideration under usual asylum application mechanisms might be appropriate. Different countries responded in different ways. Later there was a request for places to be offered to ex-detainees and exceptionally vulnerable persons, including medical evacuees, from Bosnia Herzegovina who were in need of international protection. Many countries offered places to these people, although there was a variety of approaches adopted in determining the status of those vulnerable people in the host country.

The majority of citizens of former Yugoslav states in **Austria** benefit from a form of exceptional leave to remain, whereby their tourist visas are extended while it is considered unsafe for them to return. Asylum may be applied for if the person so wishes. As of March 1993, it was estimated that Austria was host to up to 68,000 people from former Yugoslavia. Of these, 45,620 had exceptional leave to remain, 3,166 had applied for asylum, between 12,000 and 20,000 were believed to be in the country without being registered, and 200 places had been offered for ex-detainees and vulnerable persons, plus their family members.[49]

Belgium introduced a temporary humanitarian 'displaced person status', for people coming from conflict areas, or for ethnic minorities. This was restricted in September 1993 so that it would normally only be granted to people from Bosnia Herzegovina, and in March 1995 was further restricted so that it could only be granted to people from Bosnia Herzegovina. People from former Yugoslavia were able to apply for asylum through the usual mechanisms, although applications were frozen pending the ending of hostilities.[50] Between September 1992 and the end of 1995, the status of 'displaced person'

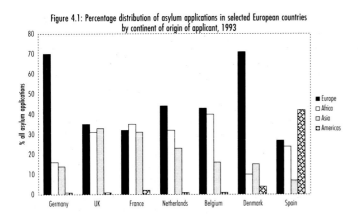

Figure 4.1: Percentage distribution of asylum applications in selected European countries by continent of origin of applicant, 1993

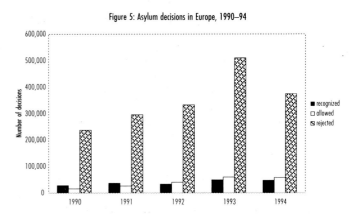

Figure 5: Asylum decisions in Europe, 1990–94

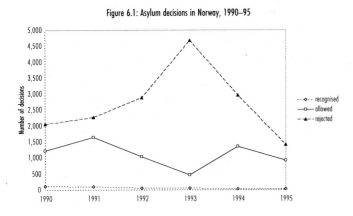

Figure 6.1: Asylum decisions in Norway, 1990–95

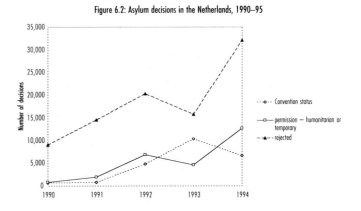

Figure 6.2: Asylum decisions in the Netherlands, 1990–95

Figure 6.3: Percentage of applications leading to recognition as a refugee in France, 1980–95

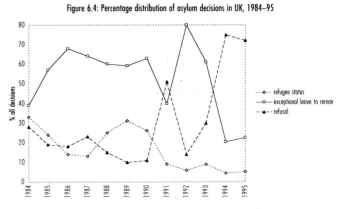

Figure 6.4: Percentage distribution of asylum decisions in UK, 1984–95

Table 2: Largest groups of asylum seekers in selected European countries, 1992 and 1995

Belgium		Denmark		France	
1992	*1995*	*1992*	*1995*	*1992*	*1995*
Zaire	former Yugoslavia	former Yugoslavia	Somalia	Turkey	Romania
Romania	Zaire	Iraq	former Yugoslavia	Zaire	Algeria
former Yugoslavia	Romania	Somalia	Iraq	Sri Lanka	China
India	Turkey	former USSR	Palestine	Mali	Turkey
Ghana	Armenia	Sri Lanka	Afghanistan	Romania	former Yugoslavia

Germany		Spain		UK	
1992	*1995*	*1992*	*1995*	*1992*	*1995*
former Yugoslavia	former Yugoslavia	Peru	Romania	former Yugoslavia	
Romania	Turkey	Poland	Cuba	Sri Lanka	N/A
Bulgaria	Afghanistan	Dominican Republic	Iran	Turkey	
Turkey	Iraq	Senegal	Equatorial Guinea	Pakistan	
Vietnam	Sri Lanka	Romania	Algeria	Ghana	

was granted to 5,855 people, people mainly from Bosnia Herzegovina and Kosovo.[51] There were applications for asylum from a further 9,000 people from the whole of former Yugoslavia between 1991 and 1995.[52] Belgium offered places for 200 people from Bosnia Herzegovina as a result of the request from UNHCR. In practice, the temporary protection status was abandoned.

In **Bulgaria** there were no changes in asylum legislation as a result of the crisis in former Yugoslavia, although people from former Yugoslavia who do not enter the asylum procedures can have their temporary residence permits renewed and so benefit from a form of temporary protection. At the end of 1995 there were 58 citizens of former Yugoslavia receiving temporary protection in Bulgaria. Citizens of former Yugoslavia formed the second largest group of asylum seekers in Bulgaria in 1994 and 1995, with 259 people applying for asylum during 1995, and 156 in 1994.[53]

The **Czech Republic** passed decrees in 1992 and 1993 which allowed citizens of former Yugoslavia to apply for temporary refuge instead of entering the asylum procedures, however, as of December 1993 only citizens of former Yugoslavia could make new applications. At the end of 1993, 38 people from former Yugoslavia had been recognized as refugees in the Czech Republic, and a further 2,335 people benefited from temporary protection, the majority of whom were from Bosnia Herzegovina. Temporary protection was offered to UNHCR for 500-ex-detainees and vulnerable people.[54]

Denmark amended its asylum legislation in November 1992, and there were several subsequent revisions, in order to allow invited groups to come to Denmark and to give temporary protection in Denmark to people form former Yugoslavia. An office was opened in Zagreb in September 1993 to deal with requests for temporary residence, mainly people from Bosnia Herzegovina, and by March 1995 this office had granted permits leading to the arrival of 6,280 people. There was a total of 17,600 people from former Yugoslavia in Denmark with temporary residence permits as of the end of May 1995, plus a further 1,670 granted asylum in some form. Denmark will also grant temporary residence permits to rejected asylum seekers who cannot be returned to their country of origin. Denmark offered 200 places for ex-detainees and vulnerable people.[55]

Finland enacted a Special Law in December 1992 to deal with the sudden increase in asylum claims from citizens of the former Yugoslavia. Those who arrived before July 1992 had their asylum applications frozen and were issued with temporary residence permits, although these were later made permanent. Those arriving after July 1992 had their asylum application dealt with in the usual way.[56] Those arriving under the quota for vulnerable persons are granted full refugee status. To the end of 1994, there were 2,872 applications for asylum from citizens of the former Yugoslavia in Finland, mainly from Kosovo and Bosnia Herzegovina.[57] In addition there were around 250 medical evacuation cases from former Yugoslavia, who were given permanent residence. Finland initially offered a quota of 72 place for vulnerable persons, with additional places for their families, but in 1995 agreed to offer a further 1,000 places over two years.[58]

France's asylum laws have no category of 'temporary protection' but temporary permission to stay may be given to nationals of the states of former Yugoslavia who arrived after the start of hostilities in Yugoslavia. An '*Autorisation Provisoire de Séjour*' (APS) allows for renewable visas to be issued to those from areas of conflict, so long as that conflict continues. Although the majority of APS have been granted to people from former Yugoslavia, there have also been a few cases of APS being granted to people from Algeria and Rwanda. At the end of 1992, 3,088 people benefited form APS; at the end of 1993 this figure was 4,470 people; and at the end of 1994, 1,874 people. It has been suggested that the lower figure for 1994 is due to people applying for other status and those leaving France. Between 1990 and 1994 applications for asylum were made by 7,613 people from former Yugoslavia, and of these over 3,000 have been granted refugee status. France offered 1,320 places for vulnerable persons, including their families. France estimates that 10,000–20,000 people from former Yugoslavia have arrived in France since the beginning of the conflict outside the asylum and APS framework.[59]

There is a form of temporary protection in **Germany**, which has existed for some time. Those who are not granted refuge status maybe given '*duldung*', tolerated status. This does not give the right of residence in Germany and does not allow family reunion. Since April 1995 some temporary residence permits (*Aufenthalsbefugnis*) have been issued to asylum-seekers from Bosnia Herzegovina. There are no statistics available on the number granted tolerated status or temporary residence permits. The German Ministry of the Interior says that at end of 1994 there were 350,000 civil war refugees from former Yugoslavia in Germany, of whom 270,000 were from Bosnia Herzegovina and 80,000 from Croatia.[60]

Greece does not have a temporary protection status, but rejected asylum seekers from the former Yugoslavia may be allowed to remain while hostilities continue in their home country. Greece offered 150 places for vulnerable persons.

There is no quota for the acceptance of refugees from former Yugoslavia in **Hungary**. People from former Yugoslavia may apply for asylum, and will be granted temporary protection if they request it. A total of 131 people from former Yugoslavia were granted refugee status from 1991 to the end of 1995.[61] The total number who have received temporary protection is uncertain, but temporary protection was granted to 4,425 people from former Yugoslavia in 1995.

Italy introduced legislation in September 1992 allowing people from former Yugoslavia admission to Italy under a form of temporary protection. This gave the right to work and in many cases the right to family reunion. Those admitted under this law may apply for asylum, but the rights they receive as asylum-seekers do not include family reunion nor in many cases the right to work, and few have applied for asylum.[62] To July 1995, 59,130 people from former Yugoslavia were granted temporary protection.[63] In addition rejected asylum applicants from Somalia may remain in Italy in order to work or study. Italy offered a quota of 400 places for vulnerable persons, and 166 people had entered Italy as part of the quota up to the end of 1995.

Between August 1992 and January 1995 an administrative regulation introducing a temporary protection scheme was in force in the **Netherlands** for displaced people from the former Yugoslavia, however, from April 1993 this was restricted to people from Bosnia Herzegovina. Under this scheme, those considered to be displaced people would be granted a temporary residence permit and their asylum application would be decided at a later date. Temporary protection was given to 7,198 people in 1992, of whom 2,573 were from Bosnia Herzegovina; 6,207 in 1993, of whom 4,938 were from Bosnia Herzegovina; and 8,635 in 1994, all of whom were from Bosnia Herzegovina. The Netherlands offered 800 places for vulnerable persons, including their families.[64] The Netherlands began consideration of suspended asylum applications from citizens of Bosnia Herzegovina during 1995, and in most cases full refugee status or permission to remain on humanitarian grounds was granted. However when the Dayton Accord was signed, those cases which had not been processed were suspended again, and the people concerned had their temporary status renewed.[65] The Netherlands has admitted 54 cases of medical evacuation from Bosnia Herzegovina, 212 ex-detainees, and their 265 family members.

Norway introduced collective protection for people from former Yugoslavia, and under this scheme their asylum application is suspended and the individual is given a temporary residence permit. Norway initially offered a quota of 900 places for ex-detainees and vulnerable persons plus close family members totalling some 3,200 people, and in 1995 agreed to offer a further 500 places. By the end of 1994 it was estimated that 10,000 people from Bosnia Herzegovina had arrived in Norway as a result of the crisis in former Yugoslavia, of whom 2,000 were part of the quota, and all were granted temporary protection.[66] During 1995 a further 1,850 people from Bosnia Herzegovina arrived in Norway, of whom 1,200 were part of the quota and 600 were arriving for family reunion.[67]

Spain amended its asylum law in May 1994 to allow the possibility of temporary protection for people fleeing war situations and to allow the government to assist in the evacuation of people from their own country should the need arise. To November 1994, temporary protection was granted to 1,626 people from Bosnia Herzegovina. Some rejected asylum-seekers have also been given temporary protection. A further 600 people, ex-detainees or their family members, have been admitted as part of Spain's quota of 1,000 and have been given Convention status not temporary protection.

In June 1993 the government of **Sweden** decided that the outstanding asylum applications from citizens of Bosnia Herzegovina would be handled generously, and almost all applicants were given permanent residence permits.[68] As of December 1994 approximately 48,500 people from Bosnia Herzegovina had been issued a permanent residence permit to remain in Sweden, the vast majority on humanitarian grounds. The law on asylum was amended in July 1994 to allow the granting of temporary permits, and Sweden awarded temporary protection to 2,380 people in 1995, the majority of whom were from Bosnia Herzegovina.[69]

Switzerland decided to grant temporary residence permits to people fleeing the conflict in former Yugoslavia, however all those entering Switzerland could apply for asylum in they wished. At the end of 1994 there was a total of 4,790 recognized refugees and 20,457 persons with temporary residence permits from former Yugoslavia. Residence permits may be issued to people from states other than former Yugoslavia. Also there are thousands of people from former Yugoslavia who do not hold a residence permit.[70]

In the **UK** there were no legislative changes made as a result of the conflict in Yugoslavia, but additions to that already in existence. There already existed the status of exceptional leave to remain, which could be granted at the discretion of the Secretary of State to people who were refused refugee status to allow them to remain in the country on humanitarian grounds. This status allows an individual to work or claim benefits, but unlike refugee status family reunion may not be applied for until four years after the status has been granted and it is not possible to obtain travel documents. The status is temporary and subject to renewal, although a permanent status can be applied for after seven years. In the 10 years between 1985 and 1995, about 23,000 people were granted full refugee status, compared to over 70,000 who were not recognized as refugees but awarded exceptional leave to remain. From the start of the conflict in former Yugoslavia to the end of 1995, there were 10,735 applications for asylum made in Britain by people from the former Yugoslavia. Of these just over 300 have been granted full refugee status and just over 2,000 have been refused refugee status but granted exceptional leave to remain. In November 1992 the British government offered a quota of 1,000 places to vulnerable persons and ex-detainees plus their dependants, and to April 1996 a total of 911 people from Bosnia Herzegovina had arrived in Britain as part of this quota plus 2,130 dependants. In August 1995 a further 500 places were offered and to April 1996, 244 people had arrived. Those arriving as part of the quota have a status of temporary refuge on an exceptional basis, which is similar to exceptional leave to remain but allows family reunion immediately, and they do not need to apply for asylum to obtain this status.[71]

Decision on asylum

Decisions on asylum applications which do not result in the awarding of full Convention status do not automatically lead to the asylum-seeker's deportation. In some countries there is an alternative status which may be awarded when the asylum-seeker is deemed to be in need of protection on humanitarian grounds. **Figure 5** gives a breakdown of asylum decisions in Europe[72] between 1990 and 1994, and shows the number of asylum applications resulting in recognition as a refugee under the UN Convention, refusal of Convention status (while being allowed to remain in some other status), or rejection of the asylum application. The number of people allowed to remain refers only to those people whose asylum application results in the granting of exceptional leave to remain, *de facto* status, or some form of leave to remain on humanitarian grounds. It does not include those whose applications result in refusal of asylum status and who remain inside the country in which asylum is sought. It does not include, for example, those applicants in Germany who are refused asylum but obtain a temporary exemption from deportation (*duldung*) and so remain within Germany. In Europe as a whole, the number of decisions resulting in full Convention status had been overtaken from 1992 onwards by the number refused refugee status but given an alternative leave to remain. Details for selected European countries show that for each between 1990 and 1994, only a small minority of applications resulted in the granting of full refugee status. **Figure 6.1** shows that in Norway, a larger number were given residence permits on humanitarian grounds than were given refugee status; however an even greater number of applicants were refused either status. The pattern is similar in the Netherlands, **Figure 6.2** except for 1993 when more decisions resulted in full refugee status than temporary permission to remain or permission on humanitarian grounds. Exact numbers of decisions in France were not available, but the recognition rate, that is the decisions resulting in full refugee status as a percentage of all asylum decisions made, is shown in **Figure 6.3**. In France, despite some fluctuations the overall trend is for fewer applicants to be awarded full refugee status. Decisions made in the UK between 1990 and 1995 are shown in **Figure 6.4**. In each year between 1990 and 1995 a greater number of applicants were granted exceptional leave to remain than were given full refugee status.

In all cases, other than those coming under accelerated procedures which may be as short as 24 hours, it needs to be remembered that there is a time lag between making an asylum application and a decision being made. This time lag may last anything from a few months to several years, depending on the speed with which the receiving country processes applications and whether an appeals procedure is invoked. This means that in any given year, some of the asylum decisions taken will be concerned with applications made in the previous year or even earlier. For example, of the 27,005 decisions on asylum applications made in the UK in 1995, only 6,860 related to applications for asylum which were made in 1995, and some (55) of the decisions taken related to applications made in 1987 or earlier.[73]

The refusal of refugee status may lead to deportation, but certainly not in every case. As already mentioned rejected asylum-seekers in Germany may obtain different *de facto* statuses and remain within Germany. Information is not available on the number with this status in Germany, but it must be substantial because there were 118,000 rejected applications in 1995 compared to around 21,000 deportations. It is difficult to assess how many rejected asylum-seekers have managed to stay within Europe, because many countries do not publish statistics on the deportation of asylum-seekers.

Central and Eastern Europe

Asylum-seekers sometimes pass through one or more countries of Central or Eastern Europe on their way to Western Europe. Now, however, countries of Central and Eastern Europe are increasingly becoming countries of asylum, and only one or two are asylum producing countries. This is probably closely related to the changes in Western Europe, since it is becoming more difficult for asylum-seekers to gain entry to most Western European countries. Some Eastern European countries have signed the UN Convention on Refugees and are starting to implement legislation to deal with applications for asylum. Statistics are difficult to obtain, but there is a limited amount of information available.[74]

Applications for asylum in Hungary reached a peak of 53,359 in 1991, when over 48,000 arrived from the former Yugoslavia, but since then each year has seen a decrease in applications. The main countries of origin of asylum-seekers in Hungary since 1989 are Romania, the former Yugoslavia, and the former Soviet Union. However, the Hungarian government signed the UN Convention on Refugees but maintained the geographical reservation, so it is only possible for asylum-seekers from Europe to apply for refugee status. For those unable to apply, UNHCR may recognize refugees under the Convention and seek their resettlement in other countries, or temporary protection may be awarded. This was granted to 4,425 people in 1995, and 1,181 people in 1994, compared to 79 and 179 granted Convention status in those years.

Full information on asylum-seekers in Poland is unavailable, but a significant increase in applications for asylum was recorded in 1995 as compared with 1994. This is probably due to the border with Germany being made more secure, leading to an increase in asylum-seekers choosing to remain in Poland rather than attempt to gain entry to another country.

In the Czech Republic the recognition rate for refugees has fallen from a peak of 36.3 per cent in 1991, when there were 1,979 applications for asylum, to 9.4 per cent in 1994 (1,188 applications) and 3.7 per cent in 1995 (1,408 applications). Czech asylum law, introduced in 1991 after the government signed the UN Convention, was amended in 1994, and this probably accounts for the decrease in recognition rates. The largest numbers of applications for asylum in 1995 came from nationals of Afghanistan, Bulgaria, Iraq, Romania and the former Soviet Union.

Bulgaria signed the UN Convention on Refugees in May 1993. Since 1991, Bulgaria has seen an increase in the number of asylum-seekers. (Data is not available for earlier years.) The majority of asylum-seekers have been from Afghanistan, the former Soviet Union and the former Yugoslavia. Many applicants from Afghanistan are not new arrivals but have been in Bulgaria for some time as students.

The politics of asylum

Refugees present a complex issue, bringing into play a variety of potentially conflicting policies. Granting asylum is a human rights and humanitarian issue. But there are also security considerations and social and economic consequences, with the result that governments make political decisions about refugees which may not always accord with humanitarian principles.

It is, ultimately, the individual state which decides whether or not to grant asylum and refugee status; and decisions cannot be detached from the political considerations that a particular government holds paramount. Rates of recognition of refugees vary with regard to a combination of the country of reception,[75] the country of origin of the refugees, and the policies of the government currently in power. The nature of the government can fundamentally influence policies: for example, in the UK the then Conservative government did not accept Chilean refugees in the aftermath of the 1973 coup; between 1974 and 1979 the succeeding Labour government admitted 3,000 in an organized programme, which in turn was terminated six months after the re-election of the Conservatives in 1979.

From a foreign policy viewpoint the decision to accept refugees will be influenced by the relationship with other states, including international alliances, military pacts and trade agreements. A particular decision may be dictated by a specific set of international conditions and also by adverse publicity. Foreign policy considerations also affect decisions on individual cases, such as the Al Masari case in the UK. Information on the country of origin of applicants is partly provided by embassies whose main brief is to ensure good relations with the countries concerned, not to monitor their human rights' records.

Domestic policies and politics bring other forces to bear – at present the main concerns are related to immigration control by and security of the state. Refugees are central in many debates about immigration, but they are rarely distinguished by state authorities from immigrants. Decisions are more likely to be dictated by labour requirements than by refugees' needs for protection. States fear that the admission of a particular group of refugees may set a precedent, thus creating a 'pull effect'[76] attracting greater numbers. The country of origin and the ethnic background/'colour' of refugees also plays a part as European countries are more hesitant to accept non-'white' refugees.

Differences of opinion also exist between different departments of state. Refugee agencies know this and make use of such discrepancies, playing on inconsistencies and contradictions to promote their point of view. Such political manoeuvrings make decisions on the basis of human rights principles difficult, and multiply the possibility of variations in the interpretation of the Convention. Different national traditions in the cultural, legal and philosophical domains complicate the matter still further.

Defending the right to asylum

The right to asylum has been defended by concerned individuals and organizations and, in particular, by the organized sections of civil society which are concerned with the relationship between democratic rights, human rights and the right of asylum. Former Director of the UN Human Rights Centre, Theo Van Boven,[77] suggests that a society's degree of solidarity can be measured by its attitude towards the vulnerable and marginalized, and it is the NGOs that support their interests. Gérard Soulier argues that the right of asylum is *'preuve et garant du droit démocratique'* (proof and guarantee of democratic right), counterpoising it with the interest of states because, expressed crudely in the words of the former French Interior Minister, Charles Pasqua, *'la démocratie s'arrête ou commence la raison d'Etat'* (democracy stops where the state's reason starts).[78]

Indeed large sectors of society have supported asylum-seekers; the sanctuary movement testifies to this as well as the campaigns launched in several European countries to defend the right of asylum. Trade unions, religious groups, women's organizations and others have all made a contribution. However, society itself is not homogeneous and sections of it have sometimes turned against refugees – as in the Swiss referendum on refugees and in the town of Sjöbo in Sweden which are described below.

Restrictive trends

European governments have become concerned with the increase and unpredictability of asylum-seekers' arrivals and the 'loss of control' over their borders. This has contributed to a chain reaction of restrictive measures with the result that European countries are all displaying the same restrictive tendencies.

Economic recession and unemployment by themselves are not sufficient explanations for this trend. For example, Norway was one of the strictest countries for asylum-seekers in the early 1980s (certainly by far the strictest of Nordic states), when it had virtually no unemployment.

Others say that public opinion has put pressure on governments to tighten controls. Yet many individual members of the public or groups have defended the right of asylum. However, it is true that local populations have at times demonstrated hostility towards refugees. For example a referendum among the 15,000 residents of Sjöbo in Sweden in the late 1980s decided against the acceptance of 15 Iranian refugees. But this led to widespread national condemnation, and public support for refugees.[79] Moreover, 'public opinion' is strongly influenced by government decisions and overall by the media. Large headlines on the 'hordes of bogus refugees' are likely to trigger an adverse reaction while compassionate images on the plight of a particular group have been shown to gain public sympathy.

Whatever the reasons, governments have introduced measures to curb the number of asylum-seekers; asylum legislation has been tightened up more than once in every EU country in the last decade (with the possible exception of Ireland).

Interpreting the 1951 Convention

Restricted interpretation can be used as a means to limit the number of refugees recognized under the 1951 Convention. Discrepancies in interpretations were studied in detail in the ECRE European Lawyers Workshop on the Implementation of Article' 1a of the Geneva Convention.[80] In most European countries the rate of acceptance of refugees has decreased considerably. One lawyer argues[81] that there is excessive emphasis laid on the objective criteria, and concludes that the spirit of the Geneva Convention is no longer respected. According to the Convention the applicant has to demonstrate 'well-founded fear of persecution', and it appears that officers interviewing asylum-seekers increasingly ask them for tangible proof of persecution. Yet such proof is not always considered sufficient as evidence, illustrated in the recent case of a Cypriot who had scars from having been tortured. It was suggested that he had deliberately inflicted these injuries himself to support his asylum claim. Medical evidence later supported the asylum-seeker's claim that he had indeed been tortured.[82] In Germany the so-called 'objectivity doctrine' prevails which holds that the determining factor is whether the perpetrator of persecution was politically motivated or not. This may mean, for example, that asylum will only be granted when torture is politically motivated.[83] The EU has now agreed on an even more restrictive interpretation of Article 1a of the Convention (see below).

Whereas the rate of Convention refugee recognition has diminished, the rate of recognition of humanitarian status refugees has increased considerably. It may be either that such refugees have come to Europe in greater numbers or that people really entitled to Convention status have been transferred into the other inferior categories.

Visas and deportations

Since the 1980s, a variety of measures have been adopted in Europe with the aim of reducing the numbers of asylum-seekers. In 1995 the UK applied visa restrictions to 85 countries. These included all but two of the countries producing significant numbers of asylum applications in the UK.[84] Visa restrictions were also imposed on nationals of the former Yugoslavia by many European countries during the 1990s as refugees began to seek safety from 'ethnic cleansing'. Moreover, the EU has agreed a common visa policy and has started to draw up a list of countries whose nationals must produce a visa to come into the EU.

In some cases agreements have been struck between several countries to prevent the arrival of asylum-seekers. In the most important arrangement of this kind made in 1985, people from the Near East, Middle East and South East Asia could only receive a transit visa from the former German Democratic Republic if they had a valid entry visa for Denmark or Sweden.[85] In 1987 an agreement between the former East and West Germany closed the 'Berlin gap' through which asylum-seekers entered Western Europe.

Visa requirements have been strengthened by the legislation providing for fines on airlines or other transporters. Some states felt that the Chicago Convention on International Civil Aviation, which makes airline companies responsible for the cost of flying back passengers without valid papers, was insufficient. Denmark (October 1988 amendment of the Aliens Act), Germany (since 1986) and UK (the May 1987 Carriers Liability Act) imposed heavy fines on companies carrying undocumented passengers. In Germany repeated offences may lead to a company losing its license to fly certain routes. While governments may argue that these measures are not aimed at asylum-seekers but are designed to control immigration, it remains evident that asylum-seekers are most seriously affected as it is more difficult for many of them to obtain valid passports and visas.[86] This has become even more watertight as the Dublin and Schengen Conventions (see below) include sanctions to transporters.

In some cases visitors requesting entry into a country have to show a return ticket and sufficient money to cover their stay; these were requirements imposed by Spain in 1989 because it found it politically difficult to impose visas on Latin American countries with which it maintains special relations. It is alleged that 30,000 Latin Americans were refused entry to Spain in 1989 and 1990 until a protest was raised by NGOs and Latin American governments.

On other occasions, police have examined passports on aeroplanes, prevented potential asylum-seekers from leaving the plane, or stopped them from leaving the international area of the airport. This prevents people from making an application which the governments in question argue can only be done on national territory. If asylum-seekers manage to reach Europe despite these hurdles, they may still be sent back without being given a chance to make a proper application, and it is believed that a number of refugees are sent back secretly.

Increasingly, however, asylum-seekers are being returned to so-called 'countries of first asylum' where they risk being sent back to the country from which they fled. If an asylum-seeker has passed through a country where they are deemed to have been able to find protection, their application may not be accepted when they arrive in Europe. Austria, Belgium, Denmark, Switzerland, Sweden and the UK have integrated the principle of 'country of first asylum' with their legislation on asylum, although they do not implement it in the same manner. In Belgium and the Netherlands, the asylum-seeker must not have stayed more than three months in a first asylum country to be eligible to apply for asylum; and in Germany, staying more than three months in another country may provide a reason for rejection at the German border. The principle of 'country of first asylum' is interpreted very strictly in Norway and Denmark; in the latter, according to amendments to the Act of October 1986, one hour in transit is sufficient for the rule of 'country of first asylum' to be applied, which entails the return of the asylum-seeker to the country of transit. This notion has been adopted by the EU (see below) and in the 1990s it prevails in Western, Central and Eastern Europe. Difficulties arise if the country to which the asylum-seeker is returned is not 'safe'. In 1992 a Tamil asylum-seeker arrived in the UK via Italy. He was returned to Italy on the 'safe country' principle, where it appears that he was refused the opportunity to make an asylum claim. He was deported to Thailand where he was detained for many months.[87]

Refugees recognized under the 1951 Convention have also been expelled. In one of the most extreme cases 10 Iranian and one Turkish refugee together with four asylum-seekers and two foreign residents were removed from France to Gabon in December 1987. After a massive public outcry from within France and abroad they were allowed to return.[88] States have even extradited refugees or asylum-seekers although it appears to contravene the non-*refoulement* clause of the Geneva Convention. Between 19 July 1986 and 11 March 1987, France extradited 50 Spanish Basques to Spain where they were apprehended by the police and kept in custody for questioning. Some have since testified to Amnesty International that they were tortured.[89] As the result of a ruling by the Conseil d'Etat in April 1988 that a statutory refugee cannot be extradited to their country of origin, such actions are no longer possible.[90]

When refugees do finally get into a European country, they may find that making an application for asylum is far from easy. In Switzerland, for example, there are only four border points at which an application can be made. In many countries a lack of interpreters can delay an application for so long that the legal deadlines have expired before it can be presented.[91]

Deterrence

A number of so-called 'deterrence measures' have been introduced to discourage asylum-seekers from coming to particular countries. One set of measures limits asylum-seekers' freedom of movement in the country, another deterrent is the use of detention. Although most European countries have legal provisions for detention these have not been extensively used except in Denmark, Finland and the UK. In February 1994, 720 asylum-seekers were detained in the UK.[92]

Indeed the position is worst in the UK where as a group, asylum-seekers 'spend longer in prison than anyone else held under Immigration Act powers'.[93] They are detained in Campsfield Detention Centre near Oxford, in conditions which are worse than those of common law detainees in prisons. They are also detained in other detention centres such as Harmondsworth (near Heathrow airport) which can hold 96 people, or in ordinary prisons when the centres are full. Asylum-seekers were also kept for a time on a car-ferry off of Harwich, the *Earl William*, which almost capsized when the hurricane of October 1987 broke the boat's moorings and swept it onto the high seas – its inmates were transferred onto land

after this incident. However, this incident does not appear to impede a new plan to buy a prison boat in 1997.

Furthermore, the use of detention is growing. In Sweden, some detentions have involved the division of families and the detention of children. This has raised humanitarian and legal concerns,[94] which have been dealt with in the 1989 Swedish Aliens Act.

One EU Resolution (1992), includes measures which make it possible to restrict the freedom of people deemed liable to expulsions, such as asylum-seekers. The movements of asylum-seekers may also be limited in other ways. These have included, compulsory housing schemes, prohibitions on employment, restrictions on welfare benefits – all of which can be considered a clear deterrent for asylum-seekers.[95]

De facto or humanitarian status refugees have even fewer rights. In Germany the *de facto* or humanitarian status does not include family reunification provisions. In the UK changes have been introduced regarding exceptional leave to remain which can be deemed to constitute deterrence: refugees will have to wait for four years before they can be joined by their spouses or children; and they will have to live in the UK for seven years instead of four before they can apply for permanent residence. In Norway the vast majority of refugees, who are granted residence on humanitarian grounds, will have to prove that they can support their families before they are allowed in to the country.[96]

Specific origins, specific destinations

Some European countries have been faced with particular refugee problems which are not relevant to other European states. In Greece, Portugal and Spain, many nationals who had been refugees elsewhere have now returned. France and Spain have been involved in both open and secret negotiations on Spanish Basque refugees in France. Austria and Italy have granted temporary asylum to people who were supposed to be settled in other countries.[97] These latter countries as well as Greece are traditionally transit countries but this situation is changing as asylum-seekers find it increasingly difficult to move on.[98]

The UK has been closely involved with the situation of Vietnamese refugees in Hong Kong, and with the potential exodus which may result when the colony reverts to China in 1997, a situation exacerbated by the crushing of the student protests in China in June 1989. The situation of the Vietnamese refugees provoked an international outcry when the British government forcibly repatriated some 50 asylum-seekers from Hong Kong in late 1989. Furthermore, the reception given to asylum-seekers from the UK's former colony, Nigeria, has been less than welcoming, with only 1 per cent granted refugee status in 1995, despite considerable evidence of human rights abuses.[99]

Germany's attitude to refugees is affected considerably by its commitment to assist and absorb ethnic Germans from other parts of Europe. In addition to the large number of asylum applications it receives from outside Europe, Germany has absorbed a large number of East Germans and people of German descent from Central and Eastern Europe.

Serious criticisms have been raised by NGOs and lawyers on issues including: the secrecy which surrounds the formulation of intergovernmental conventions and guidelines, the border discussions on asylum, the combination of visas and transporters' sanctions, the restrictive interpretations of the Geneva Convention definition, *refoulement* to 'first countries of asylum', the detention of asylum-seekers, and, more recently, possible forcible repatriation to former Yugoslavia.[100]

Refugees in Central and Eastern Europe

Until 1989 Central and Eastern Europe were seen primarily as a source of refugees moving west, often on their way to the USA. After the large scale movements from Hungary and the former Czechoslovakia in 1956 and 1968, the only similar exodus had been Poles who left after the imposition of martial law in 1981. Most other refugees were individual dissidents, who were generally given refugee status in Western Europe. However, there were wide variations in the treatment of the new Polish refugees. Very few were accepted as refugees in countries such as the UK where traditionally they had been warmly welcomed. The new Western European attitudes to refugees was also applied to East Europeans in the 1990s when they moved in large numbers, as well as refugees from 'developing' countries.

But the end of the 1980s brought new challenges to the international refugee system, making Europe once again the focus of actual and potential mass movements. Changes within Central and Eastern Europe exploded in late 1989 and early 1990. Economic stalemate combined with social discontent to bring about the collapse of the Soviet Union and the 'velvet resolutions' of the former one-party communist states in most of the region; in the former Yugoslavia a mass exodus was caused by the civil war.

The Western media has mainly portrayed the West as a place of abundance and freedom. With the difficult economic situation and shortages in consumer goods, Central and Eastern Europeans have been attracted both to potential economic betterment and to greater political freedoms. These 'pull factors' have undoubtedly had a strong influence on the decision of many people to seek refuge in the wealthier parts of Europe. Yet, destabilization of the former communist system has brought to the fore old national, ethnic and religious tensions. Unresolved by the treaties and agreements following the two World Wars, and suppressed by the authoritarian regimes which followed, old conflicts have exploded violently, and the demands for changes, whether based on national or ethnic grounds, have become a source of a growing number of refugees and the potential source of major displacements in the future. Finally, the civil war in the former Yugoslavia generated 3 million displaced people and refugees.

A new European asylum regime

Introduction

The new asylum regime is being formulated within the context of a profound crisis of an economic, political, social and ideological character in the 'developed' world. In Europe the agenda has changed from a regime implementing a selective but integrative policy of access and full status recognition with full social rights and long-term settlement, to one which maximizes exclusion on entry and undermines status and rights with the perspective of a short-term stay for refugees. This is associated with a more comprehensive approach to asylum issues. Temporary protection is one cornerstone of the new regime in the making.

Prior to the mid-1980s it is not possible to speak of a 'European policy' on asylum and refugees. What could be identified in the way of such a policy was only a conglomerate of different national policies among European states, with many policy differences, and little in the way of harmonization. Admittedly common trends could be found but these were not derived from any concerted effort.

After the mid-1980s a process of harmonization of policies on asylum began, but at intergovernmental level within the EU. Two major events precipitated this process: the imminent Single European Act which, among other issues, prepared for the abolition of EU internal borders, and the dramatic increase of asylum-seekers arriving in Europe at a time when the economic recession made newcomers 'unwelcome'. The initiatives taken in the wake of this are far-reaching; indeed they are still being pursued and expanded. Convergence, restriction and secrecy is the paradigm prevailing in this phase of European policies.

It has to be noted that the question of asylum, hardly raised at intergovernmental and international meetings in Europe in the early 1980s, has grown to become one of the central issues deserving special declarations, resolutions and policy formulation. All the main European bodies have taken it up and some were created specially for that purpose. Asylum also occupies an increasingly prominent place on the agenda of human rights organizations and religious groups.

The first structure set up to harmonize policies on asylum, drafted the Schengen Agreement, which generated a centripetal movement. All the 12 members of the EU developed similar initiatives which former European Free Trade Association (EFTA) countries are presently eager to join, signing parallel treaties on asylum and immigration. It means that all the European countries which do not produce refugees at present and are not likely to do so in the foreseeable future are to be associated in this harmonization process.

A further, and major, development at the very beginning of the 1990s, was the huge upheaval which altered the map of Europe and had a profound impact on asylum issues: namely the dismantling of communist regimes. On the one hand, it produced the lifting of controls from the former Eastern bloc. On the other hand, the crises and conflicts which ensued produced a mass refugee movement from former Yugoslavia. This was accompanied by the threat of population movements from other parts, after refugees from Central and Eastern Europe had lost their former 'legitimacy' and the favourable bias which the Cold War had awarded them, and had largely stopped coming to Western Europe. This has prompted a variety of initiatives from the EU with a view to containing refugees, which will be studied in the following sections. The new restrictive paradigm has thus become fully established. The growth of racism and xenophobia in Europe has arguably produced another momentum to restrict asylum.

Schengen and Dublin

Vast discrepancies in law, procedure, and traditions have resulted in tremendous inconsistencies in refugee policies and practice throughout Europe. Concerned about the imbalances and injustices created by the current situation, the Council of Europe and UNHCR have attempted to tackle the problem. The Council of Europe produced its first Recommendation on Harmonization in 1976 and a second on the Harmonization of National Procedure related to Asylum in 1981. The latter does not propose any formal system, but invites European states to check that their procedures and practices meet with standards recommended by the Council of Europe which require: an 'objective and impartial judgement', referral of the decision to a 'central authority', 'clear instructions' to immigration officers against *refoulement*, and permission for the application to remain while the asylum request is being examined.[101]

In the mid-1980s governments concluded that they needed to harmonize their asylum policy. However their proposals were not in accordance with the human rights standards as described by the Council of Europe guidelines; the main thrust of their discussions concentrated on measures to reduce the number of asylum-seekers and refugees in Europe at almost any cost. As individual countries have introduced restrictive measures, refugees have been diverted to those with more open policies. The main purpose of the harmonization attempts by the EU seems to have been to uniformly increase restrictions.

This harmonization project is not devoid of conflicts. States have specific national interests and some groups of countries share common views opposed to those of other groups. A clear north-south split divides Europe on the issue of refugees. As previously mentioned, the southern European states have traditionally been points of entry and transit countries for asylum-seekers – many of whom tend to move north to find better conditions of settlement. Moreover Italy had entered a reservation to its signature of the 1967 Protocol which meant that it did not recognize non-European refugees until 1990. However, northern states want their southern neighbours to make themselves responsible for, and settle, the refugees who arrive on their territories.

The Convention applying the Schengen Agreement of 14 June 1985[102] was signed on 19 June 1990 by the founder members Belgium, France, Germany, the Netherlands and Luxembourg – and instruments permitting accession to the Treaty were signed by Italy on 27 November 1990, by Spain and Portugal on 25 June 1991 and Greece on 6 November 1992. The Convention had to be ratified by all member states before it could become operational, and prior to this national laws had to be modified to enable its implementation. The Convention which came into force on 1 September 1993 was to be applied from 26 March 1996. Negotiations are taking place on the adherence of Denmark, Finland, Iceland, Norway and Sweden.

The Dublin Convention determining the state responsible for examining applications for asylum lodged in one of the EU member states, and which will supersede Schengen regarding asylum, was signed in Dublin on 15 June 1990 by all the EU members. It will come into force when Ireland ratifies it (possibly in 1997). The Convention on the crossing of external borders had not been signed by the end of 1996.

Considering an application for asylum

A central issue has been to establish which state is responsible for examining a specific asylum request. In order to avoid multiple applications, it was agreed that an application for asylum should be considered only by one state.

Governments retained as a guideline the notion of 'country of first asylum'. To define beyond doubt what this meant, the elucidation put forward was that: 'The more one state manifested its agreement to the arrival or even to the stay of an asylum-seeker, the more this state became responsible.[103] Granting a visa was deemed to be the most crucial indicator. The Schengen Group and the EU (Dublin Convention) expressed similar opinions on this. The proposed rules are summarized as follows:

The main criterion is which state authorized entry (Schengen Agreement Art. 30, Dublin Convention Art. 5). The state which granted a residence permit or the visa of 'longest duration' was to be deemed responsible. If a state did not require a visa it was nonetheless deemed responsible as this constituted an 'implicit agreement' to the arrival of the asylum-seeker. When a visa was valid in several countries, as is already the case in the Benelux countries, the country responsible would be the one where the asylum application was handed in. If an asylum-seeker was found in an irregular situation the first border reached would determine which state was responsible.

The Schengen and the Dublin Conventions broached the issue of expulsion in order to reinforce the question of responsibility. To this end the proposal stipulates that each state must ensure the expulsion of applicants to whom it has refused asylum, in order to prevent them from crossing into neighbouring countries. Moreover, to protect each country from the 'irresponsibility' of others, a 'readmission clause' was included in the proposals. Consequently, the country in charge of examining the application will have to take back asylum-seekers who may have entered other member countries irregularly (Schengen Agreement Art. 33, Dublin Convention Art. 10).

The Dublin Convention introduced an additional criterion to determine the state responsible for examining asylum requests, that of close family links; and a transfer of responsibility is planned if necessary. The Schengen Agreement also added that the treaty-making state that had granted refugee status and residence to an alien should be bound to take into consideration an asylum application from a member of their family if all the parties concerned agree to it. In this instance, the definition of family member includes spouse, unmarried minor children (under 18 years of age), and father and mother of unmarried minors.

It is also possible for a state, other than the one deemed responsible, to examine the request in accordance with its national procedure if it had special ties with the applicant or 'for humanitarian reasons, based in particular on family or cultural grounds' (Dublin Convention Art. 9). Within the Schengen Group it was agreed that asylum requests could be examined by a state which was not responsible 'for special reasons concerning national law'.[104]

The Schengen Agreement and the EU draft Convention on the crossing of external borders impose on air-, sea- and land-transporters the obligation of taking back immediately an alien refused entry; they must also take measures to ensure that aliens have the required documents to travel. In order to enforce this, the states concerned are expected to introduce sanctions accordingly.[105] They will also introduce penal sanctions on anyone who 'for purposes of gain' helps or tries to help an alien enter the territory without the required documents.[106]

Procedures

Procedures have not given rise to a great deal of debate, as a consensus was rapidly reached. It was agreed that national procedures should be left as they stood to handle applications. Subsequently the EU agreed on a Resolution on minimum guarantees for asylum procedures which covers the right of asylum-seekers during the examination procedures, appeal and revision of their application, manifestly unfounded asylum requests, applying at the border, unaccompanied minors, and, women.[107]

Exchange of information

The Schengen Group and the Dublin Convention prepared a detailed list of the type of information to be gathered, including general information on national procedures, statistical data on the monthly arrival of asylum-seekers and their breakdown by nationality, the emergence or significant increase of certain groups and more specific information on the countries of origin (Dublin Convention Art. 14) and on individual asylum-seekers; this also includes information on members of the family,[108] their documents, itineraries, and decisions taken about their cases. For this purpose the Schengen Information System (SIS) will be computerized.

From the point of view of the asylum-seekers, information concerning their countries of origin alone might be beneficial if it was sufficiently accurate. All other registers of data mentioned above belong to a vast police operation which appears necessary only if asylum-seekers are considered unwelcome and a 'threat' to European states.

Circulation of foreigners

A broad discrepancy exists between the views of the EU draft Convention on the crossing of external borders and the Schengen Agreement concerning the circulation of asylum-seekers and refugees within the confines of the Community.

The Schengen text treats refugees in the same way as other aliens holding a residence permit from one of the contracting states. They will be able to move freely within the borders of the Schengen states if they have a valid travel document, but will be obliged to declare themselves to the competent authorities on entry or within three days of entry (at the choice of the contracting parties).[109]

The EU draft Convention adopts a different attitude, arguing that the absence of broader checks will make it impossible to prevent asylum-seekers and refugees from circulating, concluding that it is best to try and put some order into their movements. Refugees would be allowed to stay in another EU state for up to three months without a visa, and asylum-seekers who cross an internal border must register with the police or relevant authorities within 72 hours.

All documents constituting the basis for these agreements were being kept confidential while they were discussed internally as well as details of the meetings of the Schengen Group and the EU which remained shrouded in secrecy.

The Steering Group on Asylum and Immigration (previously the Ad Hoc Group on Immigration)[110] continued and intensified its work after the drafting of the Dublin Convention and came up with recommendations for approval by the ministers for immigration. There is a marked contrast between the laboriousness associated with the drawing up and signing of the conventions mentioned above and the speed and efficiency of the Steering Group in passing subsequent resolutions and recommendations. Whereas the Schengen and Dublin Conventions took about five years to be completed and were still not yet implemented by all concerned at the end of 1996, several resolutions and conclusions have been agreed and been approved by the Council of Ministers. They do not have the same status as the conventions mentioned above and are not legally binding but Ministers agree to incorporate them into their national legislation and guidelines. This is a much speedier process than the process leading to the ratification of a convention and requires no discussion in national parliaments. The character of the Steering Group did not make it accountable to any EU institution.

The Steering Group submitted a programme of work which was approved at the Maastricht Summit in 1992 establishing the foundation of the EU and they have been following it through. In theory, the main aim of the Steering Group is to regulate and control immigration into the Community, which in their view means guarding external borders on questions of security and immigration.[111] In practice it has meant that priorities were largely dictated by measures believed necessary for the implementation of the Dublin Convention (see later) and the forthcoming Convention on the crossing of external borders, which had not been signed by the end of 1996. These Conventions directly placed a number of issues on the agenda which needed to be resolved before their implementation could even be considered; this is the case for manifestly unfounded applications, host third country (often called first country of asylum), countries where there is no serious risk of persecution, expulsions and visas as they require clarification and agreement. Others, such as a clearing house on asylum, and a centre for information, discussion and exchange on the crossing of frontiers and immigration, follow from the tasks stated in the conventions. Some of these are examined in more detail below. Currently, new texts are being discussed which may be incorporated into the Treaty on European Union. However these texts are likely to be seriously modified before the Inter-governmental Conference completes its work.

After Schengen and Dublin

The Resolution on manifestly unfounded applications for asylum

This Resolution was approved in 1992 at the meeting of the EU ministers during the UK presidency for immigration (30 November to 1 December 1992) and states that applications for asylum will be considered as manifestly unfounded when they raise no substantive issue under the Geneva Convention and New York Protocol for one of the following reasons: 'There is clearly no substance to the applicant's claim to fear persecution in his [sic] own country' or, 'the claim is based on deliberate deception or is an abuse of asylum procedures' (both Article 1a).

In considering this Resolution the key question to be asked is whether *bona fide* refugees are given real opportunities to be recognized even though they may find themselves channelled into an accelerated procedure because their application appeared to be manifestly unfounded. However, if an overwhelming interest in reducing the entry of refugees was to underpin implementation, this Resolution gives the authorities plenty of opportunities to invalidate an application on grounds of form rather than content.

The Resolution on a harmonized approach to questions concerning host third countries

The substance of an applicant's claim is not considered relevant (paragraph 1). Cases will be channelled into the accelerated procedure and the application may not be examined at all by a certain EU state if a third host country is identified. The danger for asylum-seekers was shown in the practice of those countries which send them back in a chain process, which ends in their return to the country where they feared persecution.

The Conclusions on countries in which there is generally no serious risk of persecution

These Conclusions are also brought about by the Resolution on manifestly unfounded applications which includes a reference to this concept. These Conclusions appear to have given rise to controversies and disagreements. In the first place the intended plan was to establish a common list of such countries for all the EU member states; it was abandoned because: 'The majority of delegations voiced misgivings for political or diplomatic reasons, or because absence from a list might imply that the country was unsafe'.[112] Instead the Conclusions provide guidelines to each individual state in assessing which countries could be considered to generally have no risk of persecution and will, through an exchange of information, reach 'a common assessment of certain countries' (Conclusions on Countries). However, some countries such as Germany, the Netherlands and the UK have already drawn up lists of such countries. It also appears that the drawing up of an EU common list was foreseen in 1996.

The elements to be considered in the assessment of these countries 'should be taken together', and include: previous numbers of refugees and recognition rates; observance of human rights, formally and in practice; the existence of democratic institutions; and stability. Nationals of countries on these lists suffer from a negative assumption which prejudices their case, especially if they are channelled on a fast track procedure.

The Resolution on the harmonization of national policies on family reunification

This Resolution applies to people who are lawfully resident with the expectation of a long-term stay but not to Convention status refugees for whom national guidelines generally already exist. However, it concerns many other refugees granted another status. It appears to be very severe and seems to reduce the possibility of family reunification to the most restrictive practices existing in Europe.[113]

Recommendation regarding practices followed by member states on the expulsion of people lawfully present in their territory

This is not specifically designed for asylum-seekers but may apply to them in some cases. It concerns people who 'have entered or remained unlawfully', which involves grounds of public safety or national security, or who 'have failed definitively on an application for asylum' without having any other claim to stay.[114] Moreover, measures are included to make it possible to restrict the freedom of

those liable to expulsion (section II), for the identification and documentation of the people concerned (section III) and for the prosecution of people who facilitate or harbour illegal entrants as well as those who employ them (sections V and VI). Readmission agreements are to be made and the agreement between Poland and the Schengen states is cited as a model (section IV).

Recommendation concerning checks on and expulsion of third country nationals residing or working without authorization[115]

This Recommendation was approved at Copenhagen (1–2 June 1993). Again this does not specifically target asylum-seekers but could affect them greatly. The strongest impact of this Resolution is probably the checks it introduces on people who are 'known or suspected of working without authority including persons whose request for asylum has been rejected'. Asylum-seekers may be concerned because they are not allowed to work in several European states, despite the fact that international human rights instruments are quoted. In any case these measures will have a profound influence on issues pertaining to personal liberty and democratic rights.[116]

Resolution on minimum guarantees for asylum procedure

This new Resolution was produced by the Steering Group after the signing of the Treaty on European Union. It covers the right of asylum-seekers during the procedure of determination, appeal and revision of their application, manifestly unfounded asylum requests, applying at the border, and unaccompanied minors and women.[117] ECRE and Amnesty International forwarded an immediate response to warn that the Resolution fell short of international standards in the exceptions which it permitted: on the suspensive effect of an appeal, and on the principle that decisions on asylum claims must be taken by a central competent authority and on nationals of other EU member states. Furthermore, concern is expressed on the notion of 'third host country' which in this instance is deemed to lead possibly to orbit situations or chain deportation.[118]

The EU interpretation of the 1951 Convention definition

The most prominent measure taken by the EU (under the Treaty on European Union) is the Joint Position on the harmonized application of the definition of the term 'refugee' in Article 1 of the 1951 Geneva Convention. It deals, among other issues, with the determination of refugee status, i.e. criteria and individual/collective determination, the establishment of evidence, the meaning and source of persecution, situations of civil war and internal conflicts, relocation within the country of origin, *refugee sur place*,[119] conscientious objection, and cessation of refugee status. This document and the draft which led to its finalization have attracted many comments and criticisms from various bodies including UNHCR, ECRE and the Dutch Standing Committee of experts in international immigration, refugee and criminal law. They challenge the limitation awarding refugee status only to people suffering persecution by the state or with the state's tolerance or complicity. EU member states do not accept the claim of somebody who is persecuted by a third party and whom the state is *unable* to protect (author's emphasis). UNHCR demonstrates that this notion is nowhere stipulated by the 1951 Convention,[120] while ECRE and the Standing Committee give examples of five European countries where jurisprudence has not adopted this interpretation.[121]

Another contentious question is that of relocation within the country of origin (internal flight alternatives). Safeguards are needed to accompany this notion: it cannot apply in the case of state persecution, the route and escape must be safe and accessible, but ECRE warns that it must also offer a durable solution with the possibility for the people concerned to settle down and earn a living.[122] UNHCR also warns that a decision concerning the existence of an internal flight alternative (i.e. within the country of origin), 'should be based on a profound knowledge and evaluation of the prevailing security, political and social conditions in that part of the country' and should not be applied in the framework of accelerated procedures.[123]

With regard to civil war and other internal or generalized armed conflicts, UNHCR and ECRE stress that the determining factor must always concern whether the asylum-seeker has a well founded fear of persecution based on one of the reasons stated in Article 1a of the refugee definition, independently of the state of peace or war in their country of origin. A final remark must be made concerning this harmonized application of the definition, nowhere does it refer to *de facto* refugees nor does it open the possibility of any additional text concerning them, while permitting the heterogeneous practices of states in this respect.

Resolution on burden-sharing with regard to the admission and residence of displaced persons on a temporary basis (25 September 1995).

This Resolution makes provisions to take into account prior contributions made by member states in the prevention or resolution of the crisis, and factors which affect their capacity for reception. It is very broad and difficulties in its implementation can be anticipated. However it establishes the long-term position of the EU on temporary protection and is clearly designed for any possible future crises.

In the period following the Schengen and Dublin agreements, EU states seem to be preparing a comprehensive and long-term strategy with the aim of restricting asylum through cooperation and harmonization of policies. The first and main leg of this strategy relates to controls and restrictions on entry. This is demonstrated by the list of priorities established in the Ad Hoc Group report

(Steering Group) submitted to the Maastricht Summit and the progress made by the Steering Group in tackling these priorities. The one area selected for a 'rapid and deep-going' harmonization is that of asylum.[124]

The policy changes connected with control and restrictions and the work related to them is well advanced, as indicated by the resolutions and recommendations studied above: the application of the Dublin Convention, the harmonization of substantive asylum law, the harmonization of expulsion policy, a clearing house, legal questions, and conditions for receiving applications for asylum. More general issues which have been dealt with are guidelines on expulsions, illegal immigration, visas and readmission agreements with other countries. Each of the measures taken to date addresses the question of control and restriction of admissions. This includes restrictions regarding access to asylum procedures. Visa requirements combine with carrier sanctions to make it extremely difficult for refugees to use their fundamental right to seek asylum. The Schengen Agreement and the Dublin Convention ensure that carrier sanctions will be introduced in all EU states and this process has already started. At the same time a common list of countries whose nationals need visas to enter all EU states does not allow for any flexibility. A tight and complete body of measures is being built up, as demonstrated by the frequent cross-references to resolutions and conventions.

The Treaty on European Union, old definitions and new concepts

The institutional framework for dealing with asylum policies in EU countries may change in the future. It appears that intergovernmental agreements might no longer be a major mechanism for harmonization of asylum in the EU; this has important implications for the openness of the debate. The greater measure of openness and consultation with the Commission (and to a lesser extent with the European Parliament) follows from the Treaty on European Union. The latter defines three areas of competence called pillars. The first pillar, on community matters, includes the determination of third country nationals needing a visa and the adoption of a uniform format for visas, for which the Commission has the right of initiative and the Parliament that of being consulted. The second pillar, on common foreign and security policy, does not mention asylum and immigration issues specifically but these are likely to be broached under its auspices. In this sphere the Commission is to be 'fully associated' with the Council's work and the European Parliament is to be informed and consulted on basic choices in policy.

The third pillar deals with justice and home affairs, and devotes a good deal of attention to immigration and asylum issues. In this area the Commission has a shared initiative with member states and the European Parliament is to be informed and consulted, although this does not appear to happen. There is a possibility of transferring some questions from the third to the first pillar – as advo-

II	I	III
SECOND PILLAR	**FIRST PILLAR**	**THIRD PILLAR**
Common Foreign and Security Policy	**European Community**	**Justice and Home Affairs**
Common Defence (Western European Union)	Area without Internal Frontiers	**ASYLUM**
• Indirect relevance to asylum matters	Economic and Monetary Union	Immigration
	Economic and Social Cohesion	Control on External Borders
	Citizenship of Union	Police, Judicial, Customs Cooperation
	• Aspects of visa policy	
	• Development cooperation	
Title V of TEU	Title II of TEU	Title VI of TEU

Source: The Refugee Council

cated by many NGOs – i.e. under community competence through a system of *'passerelle'* (transfer).

During 1996, governments in the EU seemed reluctant to bring immigration and asylum issues under the first pillar of EU matters. But the European Parliament does not appear to be ready to relinquish its right to be consulted (although again, this does not appear to be happening). As for the European Commission it intends to fully make use of its right of initiative and put forward a variety of comprehensive proposals on asylum and immigration.[125] Moreover it insists on preparing a report on the transferring of asylum matters at least, from the third to the first pillar (which would be supported by many NGOs). A tug-of-war is thus being waged among the different EU institutions over the control of asylum issues.

Central and Eastern Europe

Central and Eastern Europe represents a substantial challenge to the EU regarding asylum. The situation which prevailed in the 1980s has altered dramatically. Most Eastern European borders were closed under communist regimes and few people succeeded in getting out.

The dominant Cold War ideology made it easy for these people to be recognized as refugees in the West. In the 1990s all this has changed. The dismantlement of communist regimes had enormous consequences for refugee and asylum issues in Europe. When the demise of these governments started, mass movements of refugees crossed borders or took refuge in foreign embassies. Borders are now open and Central and Eastern Europeans can travel. But Western European government are much less keen to accept them because their numbers have risen dramatically and no ideological gain can warrant their acceptance now that the Cold War has ended. Their concern is enhanced by the realities and threats which ethnic strife and general upheavals pose in terms of population movement in these regions.

Several initiatives are being taken to deal with this situation: one question is that of asylum-seekers coming from countries bordering the EU or EU-EFTA states who might cross into these countries. Another issue is that of asylum-seekers originating from elsewhere and passing through a Central or Eastern European state before entering a Western one.

One measure designed to control entry has been to impose visas on nationals of Central and Eastern European countries, such as Bosnians and Bulgarians, in particular when they are producing or likely to produce population movements. Another has been to prepare readmission agreements with those countries. Under Germany's leadership the Schengen Group has already taken measures to deal with these possibilities and signed a Protocol of readmission with Poland and other neighbouring states in March 1991.

Where former Yugoslavia is concerned more specific decisions were taken. However, the level of coordinated response and 'burden'-sharing for the admission of refugees from that region remained disproportionately low and slow relative to the scale of the crisis.

On 30 November 1992, EU states adopted a 'Conclusion on people displaced by the conflict in the former Yugoslavia'. It is worth noting that since then more than 90,000 former Yugoslavians have applied for asylum in Germany and their number later rose to 300,000. This Conclusion happened after the High Commissioner for Refugees convened the International Meeting on Humanitarian Aid for victims of the Conflict in former Yugoslavia which endorsed a seven-point humanitarian response plan on 29 July 1992.

On 1 June 1993, EU states adopted a 'Resolution on certain guidelines as regards the admission of particularly vulnerable groups of persons from the former Yugoslavia'. By then there were 3 million displaced people from the former Yugoslavia, more than 2 million of whom had remained within ex-Yugoslav territory, while 650,000 were outside the territory of the former Yugoslavia as refugees. It is clear that the initiative and the relief efforts have rested overwhelmingly with UNHCR and NGOs, despite the European character of the crisis which could have warranted decisive action from the bulk of Western European countries and particularly from the EU states. The crisis in the former Yugoslavia has brought about a new arsenal of concepts and practices among Western countries' asylum policies.

Internalization

The notion of internalizing refugees means keeping them within their area of origin. In Bosnia Herzegovina,[126] 'safe havens' were created to be guaranteed by and under the supervision of the UN although initially it had not favoured this option. However, as tragically demonstrated in Zebrenica in 1995, 'safe havens' are perceived by all concerned as unsafe. In the EU conclusions and resolutions quoted above, it is declared and then emphasized that displaced people should be encouraged and helped to stay in the 'nearest safe area to their homes'. While assistance would be given to make this possible, any other alternative will be envisaged only if this proves impossible. This kind of circumscribed regionalization has attracted wider interest and was also pursued by the Inter-governmental Consultations in a substantial working paper on reception in the region of origin.[127] A trend appears to have been established.

Containment

If internalization is not possible, EU states promote containment, i.e. a narrow interpretation of regionalization, whereby refugees should remain within the territory of former Yugoslavia. Out of 3 million refugees, only 650,000 were received in countries which were not former Yugoslav territory. The EU would make 'provisions to assist with material assistance in supporting reception centres in the former Yugoslavia'. Indeed, large resources in cash and material assistance were sent out for humanitarian purposes in former Yugoslavia.[128]

Temporary protection

Finally, the main concept adopted and implemented in the case of former Yugoslavia is that of temporary protection as stipulated in the Conclusion on people displaced by the conflict, whereby EU states undertake to respect a number of guidelines including: 'Readiness to offer protection on a temporary basis to those nationals of the former Yugoslavia'.

Who is deemed to benefit from temporary protection? According to the Conclusion it must be people coming direct from combat zones, who are within an EU state border and cannot return to their homes 'as a direct result' of the 'conflict and human rights abuses'. This limits access to temporary protection considerably.

In addition, temporary protection could be offered to 'vulnerable groups', as defined by the Resolution on certain common guidelines (Copenhagen 1 June 1993). Such groups are: detainees as prisoners of war in internment camps who are at risk for 'life or limb', people in critical need of medical treatment who cannot obtain it *in situ*, those who have been subjected to severe sexual assault with no assistance possible near their home and generally those who are 'under direct threat to life or limb' and who cannot be protected otherwise. All these categories broadly meet UNHCR recommendations although they do not specifically include 'children at risk'[129] or 'persons who for other reasons specific to their personal situation are presumed to be in need of protection'.[130] The one innovation

for many states in this list concerns women subjected to sexual assault, thus creating a new category of people worthy of protection on a European scale.

This type of temporary protection differs from the temporary protection awarded in other regions of the world in situation of large-scale influx and for which the UNHCR drew up recommendations: EXCOM Conclusions No. 19 (XXXI) on Temporary refuge in 1980 and Conclusion No. 22 (XXXII) on the protection of asylum-seekers in situation of large scale influx in 1981. As pointed out by Kjaerum,[131] temporary protection had previously been perceived as an intermediate step towards a durable solution, i.e. in the country of entry or as resettlement in a third country. In the case of former Yugoslavians there has been no such perspective as the only plan seriously considered is to return refugees to their country of origin as soon as possible. 'Burden'-sharing has proved impossible; three or four countries bordering the region host 50–60 per cent of some 600,000 refugees not living in an immediate neighbouring country.[132] This has been reinforced through the introduction of visas for nationals of former Yugoslavia by most Western European states and by returns to 'first host countries' if the refugees did not arrive directly from their country of origin.

As we have seen, most European countries have made offers of temporary protection, however, large discrepancies exist where the situation of people benefiting from temporary protection is concerned. Not only does it differ according to the country of reception but conditions of reception may also vary within the same host country as a result of an arbitrary set of factors such as whether the person has been admitted under a 'vulnerable group' quota or has arrived spontaneously, whether accommodation is provided in a refugee centre or with hosts. Even access to the asylum procedure is not uniform; some countries make it available immediately upon arrival, others suspend it for a few months as in the Netherlands, or two years as in Denmark. Some refuse it altogether, making it incompatible with a temporary protection.[133]

UNHCR and NGOs are concerned that temporary protection may in practice entail the withholding of refugee status and exclusion from an integration programme. Particularly sensitive issues are those related to the access to asylum procedures, the right to family reunion, the right to work and training and to education.[134] More generally, there is a risk of setting a precedent creating second-class refugees, which would also lower protection standards for others.[135]

Finally, UNHCR has examined the position of refugees from former Yugoslavia *vis-à-vis* the Geneva Convention definition and concluded that many would qualify for refugee status. It recommends applicability of the definition to deserters and war evaders in this particular context. It refutes the argument that the situation of civil war turns people into 'war refugees', as the movements of population are not just the consequences of the war but one of its goals for the purpose of ethnic cleansing. It also argues that even if civilians are the perpetrators of these crimes the persecution is not invalidated by the fact that the legal or *de facto* power is not directly responsible as it either tolerates them or is incapable of preventing them.[136] This means that people under temporary protection would most probably have obtained Convention status if they were put through the determination procedure and is presumably one reason why they were discouraged from so doing. However, those who would not meet the Convention criteria would have been entitled to protection on humanitarian grounds. This form of temporary protection has come to stay; a temporary protection with the sole perspective of return. Already before the negotiation of the peace settlement at the end of 1995, the EU's General Affairs Council stipulated that goodwill on the part of countries of origin to accept the return of refugees was to be one of the criteria for the granting of reconstruction aid to states of former Yugoslavia.[137]

Temporary protection is a notion which has come to stay in Europe. However, many aspects of its mode of implementation are still being debated and their resolution will determine the standard of protection awarded. These include: the circumstances in which temporary protection will be deemed appropriate, the criteria for determining its beneficiaries, the duration of temporary protection status and their standard of treatment. Other questions concern the relationship of temporary protection to asylum procedures, the crucial issue of return, the 'burden'-sharing and the nature of international action about conflicts in areas of origin, which are concomitant with the concept of temporary protection.

The UNHCR

The UNHCR has been a major player in the introduction of temporary protection for displaced former Yugoslavians. Because of its policies, it has attracted sharp criticisms. From the lawyers' community, Hathaway accuses the organization of having given tacit approval to the use of temporary protection 'as an opportunity or excuse to restrict refugees' rights.[138] Concern is also voiced by ECRE with regard to temporary protection's impact on the standards of treatment for refugees in general.[139] UNHCR *realpolitik* and the apparent trading of an EU agreement to offer temporary protection to former Yugoslavians against more precarious social rights appears to be confirmed by one intergovernmental mouthpiece: 'Enhancing the rights of beneficiaries so much that the stay would become more permanent... could diminish both the capacity and willingness of states to provide such protection'.[140] Goodwin-Gill notes that changes wrought in UNHCR's mandate are leading to a lessening of protection for refugees 'substituting "humanitarian action" for the duty to provide international protection'.[141]

The UNHCR's failure to protest against *refoulement* and the promotion of repatriation in less than secure conditions might be tantamount to an abandonment of protection and of its mandate.

Conclusions

The EU, or more precisely a number of its member states, have been a driving force for the setting up of the new asylum regime. Their initiative was motivated by two interrelated factors: the will to tighten up on immigration controls and the determination to regain complete sovereignty over national borders. This explains why the Geneva Convention and its potential beneficiaries have been the main target of an intensive effort on the part of the EU, because according to the Geneva Convention to which states are signatory, refugee determination must be guided entirely by the moral claim of the applicant. Manifestly such goals could only be attained through the harmonization of policies which is a major feature of the new regime. States did not dare renege on the Convention for fear of an uproar from the organized sectors of civil society and international bodies. The chosen strategy was thus to clip its wings and reduce its scope as much as possible through intergovernmental agreements and a battery of EU resolutions, recommendations and conclusions.

The main features of the new regime examined in this section can be summarized as follows:[142]

A fundamental change takes place with regard to instruments and statuses:

- The Geneva Convention becomes a residual instrument while asylum is governed by *ad hoc* or indirect instruments giving rise to varied *ad hoc* statuses;
- The new instruments are non-binding in the shape of guidelines;
- The non-*refoulement* clause on the whole is maintained;
- Group determination in a negative ('safe country' notion) and positive (former Yugoslav vulnerable groups) manner replaces individual determination;
- Temporary protection is introduced with return as the only durable solution envisaged;
- Access to host countries and to the asylum procedure are made increasingly difficult.

The standards of treatment are severely downgraded:

- Stay becomes uncertain and short term; temporary protection makes this explicit;
- 'Non-integration' and a reduced level of social rights replace integration policies;
- Hostility and prejudices towards refugees are increased.

A 'comprehensive' approach prioritizes protection and action outside potential EU reception countries to provide help *in situ* or as close to the area of origin as possible. It also proposes repatriation combined with reconstruction programmes (in former Yugoslavia).

It was clear that protection could not be abandoned totally and that many refugees could not be returned to their place origin. *Ad hoc* statuses were implemented but the prevalent xenophobia and the anti-immigration rhetoric of governments made it difficult to offer integration in the society of reception. Other status refugees were often left in limbo about their situation apart from being allowed to remain. Temporary protection solved the dilemma: protection was granted, but for a limited period with return as the only outcome envisaged. The question of integration did not have to be posed; and family reunion was perceived as negating those premises. Moreover, the instruments adopted to govern temporary protection were guidelines, albeit on a European level and thus while furthering the harmonization process, did not impinge in any way on national sovereignty (this is stressed more than once by the Secretariat of the Inter-governmental Consultations 1995). This is why temporary protection was a major breakthrough for EU governments.

Reception and settlement policies are consistent with the new asylum regime examined above: the general assumption which underpinned policies towards facilitating a long-term stay for refugees in the old regime are reversed.

This new asylum regime is part of a new immigration regime. The plan is 'controlled managed immigration', that is the recruitment of temporary contract workers to meet the needs of the economy. These will be sent back with no possibility of settling down'; integration is definitely kept out. We are witnessing the setting up of integrated asylum and labour migration policies by governments.[143] For asylum this has meant 'the downgrading of the entire European asylum system'.[144]

▶

Settling refugees in Europe[145]

Although governments have not given priority to conditions of settlement, international conventions, refugee agencies and NGO place considerable emphasis on this area.

The 1951 Geneva Convention stipulates the obligations of states which grant refugee status and makes a number of recommendations regarding employment and welfare which include rationing, housing, education, public relief and all aspects of health and social security. The UN Universal Declaration of Human Rights also makes a case for satisfactory conditions of living, Article 25 (1) states that:

> 'Everyone has the right to a standard of living adequate for the health and well being of himself [sic] of his family, including food, clothing, housing and medical care and necessary social services, and the right to security in the event of unemployment, sickness, disability, widowhood, old age or other lack of livelihood in circumstances beyond his control.'[146]

The Declaration also includes the right to employment and education.

In Europe, both the European Parliament and the Council of Europe have concerned themselves with refugees and asylum-seekers' conditions of settlement, stressing the importance of this issue.[147] The Commission devoted a substantial section of its communication on immigration and asylum policies (1994) to reception and integration issues. Even the EU is preparing a 'plan of collective action' for minimum reception conditions for asylum-seekers.[148]

The question of settlement is a fundamental one from several points of view. First, in terms of the Geneva Convention, states undertake to meet certain minimum standards. People should not only be granted admission, but should be enabled to lead a normal life. In a paradoxical argument, lack of settlement facilities has sometimes been used as a reason for limiting the number of places offered to refugees[149] making the issue of even greater importance for them.

Satisfactory settlement is not only beneficial for refugees but also for the societies in which they settle. Positive policies enable refugees to make a contribution instead of being a potential burden. A dramatic example is that of the 15 Nobel Prizes won by refugees who have settled in the UK.[150] There are many more examples of valuable, albeit less spectacular, contributions made by refugees and these will be examined below.

Institutions, policies and issues

Several institutions have a role to play in the settlement of refugees and depending on circumstances, may interrelate more or less amicably, sometimes entering into conflict with, or simply ignoring, one another.

On the whole governments have taken few direct responsibilities in settlement other than making a financial contribution. A few have managed the reception of refugees in organized programmes. Refugee settlement falls within the remit of different ministries in different countries: The Regional Centre of Social Security of Lisbon in Portugal; the Ministry of Labour and Social Security in Spain; the Ministry of Immigration in Sweden; and several ministries in France (Social Security, Foreign Affairs, Interior Ministry).

More often than not central government has handed over total or partial responsibility for the settlement of refugees to NGOs which it helps financially: this is the case in Belgium, Denmark, France, Italy, Norway, Spain, Switzerland and the UK. This pattern has increased the discrepancies in provision as NGOs have different methods and approaches. In France, for example, they divided their responsibilities according to the task: the Croix Rouge looks after reception at airports and takes care of unaccompanied minors; the Cimade organizes language classes; and France Terre d'Asile takes charge of housing.[151] In the UK, on the other hand, the division has been territorial: in taking care of refugees from Vietnam, Ockenden Venture, Refugee Action and the British Refugee Council shared out the country by regions between themselves for several years.

The involvement of NGOs has been positive, offering greater flexibility and frequently more commitment. In addition they have been shown to organize settlement far cheaper than governments. In some cases established NGOs have been criticized for limiting their work to recognized refugees,[152] but this is no longer widespread and, in any case, alternative organizations have been created which do not discriminate between categories of refugees.

Two negative aspects of NGO work can be cited: some lack of professionalism for which goodwill cannot always compensate,[153] and occasional rivalry between agencies which does not work in the refugees' interest. Results are most positive when liaison exists between the various NGOs and with other agencies.

NGOs may be involved in the first stages of settlement and thereafter hand over the refugees to local government authorities. In every country there is a point where local authorities have to play a role although the timing varies. In

Denmark refugees whose asylum applications have been approved come under the Danish Refugee Council and their transfer to local authorities takes place 18 months later. Local government bodies may take an active role in the resettlement: in the Netherlands and Sweden they are funded for this purpose. In many countries, including the UK, lack of specific funding has made local governments reluctant to devote resources to refugees, whose needs are frequently ignored. More dramatically, in Belgium some municipalities took illegal action in refusing to register refugees on the grounds that it placed too great a 'burden' on them.[154] As a result refugees were unable to get medical care, send their children to school or receive social assistance.

A major concern is the lack of information and training for local government employees who deal with refugees. The Council of Europe Standing Conference of Local and Regional Authorities of Europe (SCLRAE) drew up recommendations on the treatment of refugees, in particular regarding appropriate training of local authority officers. It also recommended the nomination of specific local executive officers to take charge of the issues relating to refugees in each authority.[155]

Refugee associations also have a role to play in the process of settlement. Refugees have demonstrated a great ability to reconstitute their communities and have created associations that perform a variety of functions, ranging from Chilean concerts to Vietnamese New Moon festivals and Kurdish Newroz celebrations. They also offer advice and can act as mediators as well as pressure groups.

UNHCR summarized the central role played by refugee organizations in five vital areas: they help new arrivals with practical matters relating to integration; they provide psychological and material support; they help refugees maintain their cultural identity; they promote a positive image among nationals of the host countries through cultural presentations; and they provide an opportunity for meaningful activity, enhancing refugees' self-image.[156] As a result SCLRAE recommended that local authorities promote the creation of local and regional associations of refugees and cooperate with them.[157]

These initiatives have been widely welcomed, but there is a need for greater understanding of the settlement process and for policies which reflect this. A number of central issues need clarification if progress is to be made.

Settlement: the major issues

For the individual asylum-seeker the process of settlement begins on arrival. This is, however, not the view of the authorities who want to differentiate between those who will be given permission to stay and those who will not. Moreover, many countries have deliberately created poor conditions in the pre-asylum period in order to deter asylum-seekers. This policy is maintained in spite of the potential length of the waiting period and in the knowledge that it is detrimental to eventual settlement of those who are accepted, thus in their own terms increasing the 'burden' on the receiving society.[158] It is generally accepted that it is particularly important for the asylum-seeker that he or she be allowed to work as soon as possible after submitting their application.[159]

Reception centres

Most European countries have reception centres. These may occupy a motley collection of premises – old hospitals, hostels or even unused barracks. Opinions are divided as to their desirability and on the optimum length of stay. It has been argued that they are useful because they do not leave people isolated, they make it easier to distribute the necessary provisions, and allow for a medical check. They are also a relatively cheap mode of reception.

Against this it is claimed that centres isolate people from society by creating an artificial environment, and they may develop a dependency if the length of stay is prolonged.[160] In the UK, refugees from Vietnam stayed for as long as a year in centres.[161]

Another objection to reception centres is that mutually hostile communities may be housed together. In Spain one group had to be moved when Laotians and Vietnamese were housed in the same centre.[162]

Housing

Housing is a basic need, but even here there is no agreed policy or practice. Generous provision is made for public or subsidized housing in some countries. Refugees are provided with a good deal of social housing in Scandinavia, and in the Netherlands 5 per cent of all newly-built dwellings with government subsidies are annually set aside for refugees.[163] On the other hand, in Belgium, housing has to be found in the private sector. More commonly there is a combination between the two systems, as is the case in France and the UK, where housing associations have played a central role in providing housing to refugees. In most instances housing is not easy to obtain rapidly, and this is frequently a cause of prolonged stays in reception camps.

The allocation of accommodation immediately raises other questions such as the geographical location and distribution of the refugees. In Belgium a 'distribution plan' has been approved by the Conseil des Ministres establishing criteria for determining how many asylum-seekers should be allocated to particular municipalities. The criteria include the ratio of inhabitants to the national population, the relative prosperity of the municipality, and the number of asylum-seekers already assisted. This plan has, however, been partly held in check by the refusal of some municipalities to accept additional refugees.[164]

Another approach has been the dispersal policy used in the UK for the settlement of Vietnamese. The government and the relevant NGOs agreed that no more than 10 and no less than four families should be housed in the same municipality, despite the fact that the refugees themselves often expressed the wish to be housed near a 'Vietnamese community'.[165] The rationale behind this decision was that it would not 'overburden' any single local authority and would facilitate local support; it would avoid the creation of ghettos and a possible backlash on the part of local populations. Ten years later the Vietnamese refugees have regrouped in a few large centres – London, Birmingham and Manchester. This pattern of secondary migration is confirmed by studies of refugees in Canada, Sweden and the USA and indicates a need to develop policies which will take account of refugees wishes to remain together as a community.

However, if refugees are to be concentrated, the local authorities concerned will expect financial support to enable them to provide appropriate services. In the Netherlands this approach has been tried with so-called 'nuclear' municipalities. In Sweden some municipalities were asked to 'specialize' in certain ethnic groups of refugees and given a financial incentive to do so with the result that it has become easier to provide adequately trained staff and sufficient resources. A study of local and regional authorities concludes that the most desirable model is the concentration of refugees in medium-sized cities.[166] A significant benefit is that refugee communities can provide support to their members, particularly in the case of relatively homogeneous groups. An original project of housing a group of 500 Hmong and another group of 400 Hmong in French Guiana (Latin America) has shown good results.[167]

Employment

It is possible that an overriding concern for providing housing risks placing obstacles in the way of finding employment. As a rule accommodation is easier to find in areas where unemployment is high. And employment is arguably the most important single factor in successful settlement. But it is not an easy question to resolve. Refugees face major hurdles in trying to break into employment, and paradoxically, one needs to have a job in order to obtain one; an employer's reference is generally required and a positive *curriculum vitae* is necessary for an application to be successful.

Qualified people often cannot practice because there is no equivalence of degrees and qualifications, and they experience severe downward social mobility. In addition an appropriate language course is required as professional work usually requires a good knowledge of the host country's language. In some cases additional training is required to adapt expertise to a new system and new idiosyncrasies. Arrangements of this kind were made in France for Latin American social workers.[168] In other cases not being a national of the country makes it impossible to enter certain professions such as being a school teacher in France. In some cases legislation governing employment has been modified to take into account the specific situation of refugees. In French universities the rule limiting a non-national lecturer's contract to three years has been waived for Convention refugees.

Manual workers do not depend so much on language but may find that their specific skill is not needed in Europe. However, their greatest problem is the discrimination experienced by refugees, especially if they come from a 'developing' country. They are frequently offered the most menial and worst paid jobs. Although no accurate statistics are available, it is safe to say that a good number of refugees have had to take up casual undeclared employment – in catering, childcare, decorating and cleaning. Obviously refugees may succeed in moving on to regular and stable jobs and this has a value beyond its monetary reward; as one refugee said when this happened, it was as though his dignity had been given back to him.

There is some evidence that local contacts and initiatives yield the best results in providing employment opportunities.[169] Employment schemes developed by refugee workers with local employers have proved positive. In the Netherlands strong ties were established between training schemes and local employers; in Birmingham in the UK a refugee association has obtained funding for an employment development officer who builds up contacts with local employers; in France the *centres d'hébergements* have created useful links with local employers and even launched or supported job creation schemes.[170]

Self-employment projects are another possible avenue. In the south of France successful rural projects have been set up.[171] In Spain a government programme provided facilities and financial support to refugees who wanted to start a business or work on the land.[172] A few enterprises of this kind have proved successful in France and in the UK in the form of restaurants and craft shops. In the UK these started as cooperatives with loans from the Industrial Common Ownership Finance Limited – a government body for the support of workers' cooperatives – and a grant from the County Council. Many other examples can be found throughout Europe.[173]

Training schemes have sometimes led to employment, but they have also failed because they were not tailored to the needs of the trainees. Language can be a major obstacle. Vocational training has to be handled with care. It can cause greater problems if it does not lead to employment. On the whole the employment market is difficult; it is even more so for refugees. A good understanding of the local employment situation is necessary; courses have to match local labour demands and be relevant to refugee needs.

As ever, *de facto* refugees and asylum-seekers encounter the greatest difficulties. Generally they have fewer entitlements than Convention refugees. Their uncertain status arouses suspicion among employers, who are further discouraged by administrative complications and delays in obtaining work permits.

Language and education

Language is crucial to successful settlement. For young people it is the key to access to education; for adults it opens up a wide range of possibilities, not least of which is managing everyday life.

In all European countries children of refugees – with some exceptions for asylum-seekers and some temporary protection refugees – have access to free and compulsory education in schools where they are also taught the host country's language. In some countries the children can be placed in introduction classes before being integrated into the curriculum. It is too often assumed that children settle into European schools without problems. Several studies indicate that this is not always the case.[174] Refugee children would benefit if teachers were given appropriate training and information on their situation and culture. Refugee children need an explanation of the 'new system' which they may find very different from their previous experience.

For adults the difficulties are even greater and the opportunities available vary considerably throughout

Europe. In Germany adult refugees can attend free language classes, in Denmark attendance at daily language classes is a condition for obtaining welfare benefits, in France and the Netherlands refugees are offered statutory language classes.[175] In the UK refugees have not been offered special language courses except for those provided for Vietnamese in reception camps, and where courses have been set up through local initiatives. But even in countries where language courses are organized they do not necessarily meet the needs of the refugees who are not simply learning a new language but also how to function in a different society and culture.[176] In addition the wide range of languages of origin can impede satisfactory tuition and it frequently happens that people who are illiterate are placed in the same classes as those with a far higher level of educational attainment.

Other kinds of education are also important. Where training or courses are offered, grants may have to be given to enable refugees to attend, especially if they have family responsibilities. In the UK the World University Service (WUS) awarded numerous grants to refugees; in France refugees have enjoyed the statutory grants available to nationals as well as specific schemes.[177] But the problem of language has to be resolved first. Insufficient knowledge of the language is a recurrent obstacle for vocational training, further education or obtaining better employment. One aspect of education often mentioned by refugees is the possibility of preparing for a career that may be useful on their return to their own country. WUS and Cimade grants have been offered which are 'development oriented' for this purpose.

Health and social assistance

In most European countries refugees have the same welfare rights as nationals. This is not the case however for asylum-seekers and *de facto* refugees whose rights are more limited and vary greatly from country to country. Refugees sometimes also receive additional assistance during the initial period of settlement. Such assistance is currently given in France, Germany, Luxembourg and the Scandinavian countries.[178]

Social service provision is characterized by lack of training and knowledge of practitioners. SCLRAE made strong and wide-ranging recommendations on this issue.[179] Training refugees to become social workers appears to have had positive results in ensuring the delivery of services.[180]

Health issues have to be given far greater attention. Many refugees have had deeply traumatic experiences and require sensitive and prolonged counselling. This is compounded by the experience of having lost the social world to which they belonged. A good programme, which explains and demystifies the society of settlement, combined with conditions which encourage the preservation of their community, has been shown to make a positive contribution to mental health.[181]

It is important to make a distinction between mental illness and psychological and behavioural problems. An UNHCR study on the mental health of refugees in five European countries demonstrated the inappropriateness of responses to non-European refugees. Several proposals were put forward to remedy this including: greater

involvement of family and refugee associations' networks, the formation of a specialized organization of practitioners focusing on the condition of refugees and on different cultures, and good information on the services available.[182] SCLRAE recommends the creation of medical aid centres for refugees with specialists able to assist in overcoming the effects of traumatic incidents which may occur many years after the refugee has fled.[183] For counselling, good interpreters are essential and in some instances specialized people from the same community have been able to perform this function.

Temporary protection

The temporary protection concept introduced in the 1990s for the former Yugoslavia, has led to the granting of much reduced social rights for its beneficiaries. The standard of treatment reveals large discrepancies between different European countries. Those under temporary protection are not generally awarded an integration programme and are not entitled to identity/travel documents, nor to family reunion. These measures severely undermine the wellbeing of such people and have been criticized by NGOs in the reception countries where they have been implemented.

Social and cultural activities and political rights

It has been argued that the preservation of cultural identity appears to be a positive element in the integration process.[184] In the Netherlands grants are made to a few refugee associations. In Norway and Sweden, it is compulsory to organize the teaching of the language of origin to refugee children. In France, books have been reprinted in Khmer, Lao and Vietnamese, for example, with great success. Where they have not been provided, refugees have organized numerous mother tongue classes for their children. They have also promoted a wide variety of cultural functions.

Paradoxically refugees have sometimes been told that they should not get involved in political activities whereas, for many of them, the sole reason for leaving their country was their political involvement. This constitutes a major motivation to continue politics in exile, and to support the parties that have been defeated or outlawed in their homeland. In France a prohibition of this type was challenged, and the only limitation which was upheld requires refugees to respect French law in the course of their political activities.

Organizations working with refugees have continuously emphasized that refugees need to nurture their links with their homeland and with their communities in other regions or in other countries.[185] Organizations and links could be encouraged not only on a local, regional and national level but also internationally.

Naturalization

UNHCR has proposed that refugees should be given full access to naturalization as a way of belonging to and participating in the reception society without any restriction.[186] Naturalization certainly provides advantages including access to some professions barred to non-nationals in several European countries (e.g. France, Germany, Portugal and Spain), and the right to political participation. But there is more to the question than convenience. Despite the advantages to be gained many, if not most, refugees are reluctant to become naturalized or do so only after a long time in exile. Several factors shape this attitude of which the most important is loyalty to the homeland which they were forced to leave.

Public opinion

Refugees are very sensitive to public opinion. The attitude of the surrounding population affects most aspects of their everyday life and it can make the difference between a supportive, harmonious, friendly environment and unpleasant, hostile, prejudiced encounters.

The major agent shaping public opinion is the media. As a rule the media tend to report home news more than international news and to focus on sensational stories, which in practice often means negative ones. As the French adage goes 'les peuples heureux n'ont pas d'histoire' (happy people have no history). Positive stories of refugees in reception societies hit the headlines much less frequently than negative ones. On the other hand the causes of the refugees' flight are rarely presented accurately or in depth because they are not perceived as relevant to a domestic readership. The false perceptions resulting from this distortion of the refugee story are aggravated by the overwhelmingly hostile statements issued by many politicians, which are then widely covered by the media.

As a result, refugees are increasingly presented not as people in need of protection but as people who are a threat, not as people who have a problem but as people who are a problem. Large headlines proclaim that 'unjustified claims of refugee status "will not be accepted"',[187] and that there will be 'fines to halt bogus refugees'.[188] This was followed by 'airline fines have cut refugee influx' which explained that, 'The number of immigrants applying for refugee status has fallen rapidly since the government warned airlines they would be fined if they carried passengers without proper documents'.[189] The effect of such reporting is to reinforce the underlying paradigm on which government policies on asylum are based: refugees are first and foremost perceived and presented as undesirables – illegal immigrants, potential terrorists and drug dealers. This has exacerbated hostility and racism which has led to the infamous arson attacks and assaults in Germany, Switzerland and Sweden (among other countries), causing several deaths.

To counteract this 'bad press' and racism, refugee agencies have organized campaigns of public information in several European countries. The Council of Europe and UNHCR recommended that local authorities should organize publicity campaigns for refugees. Finally ECRE has warned against pernicious use of language and recommended that such terms as 'floods', 'influxes', 'torrents', 'streams', 'bogus', 'swamped', etc. should be avoided to project a more positive image of refugees.[190]

Return

Return to their country of origin is a central concern for many refugees, and the process of settlement is fundamentally affected by it. A proportion of refugees return when the circumstances that forced them to leave their homeland have changed: Argentinians, Chileans, Uruguayans. It has been shown that unsuccessful settlement frequently leads to unsuccessful returns. But it is seldom an easy process, and refugees themselves have stressed the importance of good preparation.

Refugee organizations have played an active part in preparations. For example, the Comisión de Información Sobre el Retorno Chileno in Paris held weekly sessions of advice for refugees who wanted to return home and emphasized the need for such a service.

Settlement countries could play a positive active role by reaching agreements with the countries of origin of the refugees to facilitate their return, particularly in practical matters such as pension arrangements and through restitution of civil rights. However refugee agencies insist that it must be ensured at all times that return is voluntary and that no pressure is put on refugees to return. To date such pressure has not been applied within Europe. When the situation in the refugees' homeland has changed, they have usually been allowed to stay on. In France, Argentinians who wished to remain have been given the chance to obtain French nationality when their refugee status came to an end. But the UK has been prepared to force Vietnamese refugees in Hong Kong to return to Vietnam which, taken together with adverse publicity and increasing numbers of *refoulement* cases, may herald a general change in approach.

As for refugees from the former Yugoslavia, return is the priority – sometimes the only option – when the situation in their country of origin permits.

Unaccompanied minors

The arrival of children and young people on their own is a relatively new but growing phenomenon which raises a variety of problems. Some are legal, relating to 'personal status' and guardianship. In some cases – Denmark, Iceland, Norway and the UK – they are decided in relation to the country of domicile; in others – France, Germany, Italy, Sweden and Switzerland – on the basis of nationality. A 'minor' is defined as a person under 18 in most European countries.[191]

Decisions on minor asylum-seekers are influenced by government fears that they may open the door for larger movements through family reunion. Finally the whole area of care and the best way to settle these young people still has to be explored thoroughly. Group accommodation seems to have had positive results in Denmark, Sweden and the UK.

Contributing to society

Good settlement conditions make it easier for refugees to make a positive contribution to their host society. Many do so unnoticed in a variety of ways. Refugees have become integrated into all the branches of the labour market using skills that they brought with them – Chilean miners have become coal miners in Scotland, Vietnamese tailors and jewellers have continued with their trades.

Others have learned new skills – many taxi drivers in Paris are refugees. Professionals – academics, doctors, engineers – have also made their contribution.

All adult refugees are potential contributors to their host society, which does not have to bear the cost of their education. And refugees themselves overwhelmingly want to make a contribution.

Additionally, refugees have also added new dimensions to the culture of the reception societies. Evidence of the cultural contribution is provided by the significant number of established artists. There is a growing body of literature written in exile; theatre groups are thriving from the Cypriot Teatro Technis in London to the Chilean theatre Aleph in Paris; painting and a range of musical groups add to the mix.

However the real impact is in the refugees' way of life and refugees have contributed to every walk of life, including the ideological and the political in the reception society. Many have joined trade unions; others have played an active role in political life.

Although refugees are opposed to the regimes which have forced them to flee, they act as ambassadors of the people of their country and as representatives of their culture and society. One could argue that they have helped to open minds and combat racism and prejudice. Of course not all refugees have been able to make positive contributions. There are problems in finding employment and adapting to a new society which lead to disillusion and apathy. Such cases create an image of refugees of being a 'burden' to the reception society. However, one could turn the argument on its head to conclude that, given the vast difficulties encountered by refugees, it is a testament to their strength and vitality that so many have done so well. It must be the primary objective of good settlement policies in housing, education, health and employment to create conditions which make it possible for all refugees to contribute equally with the host population. Reception strategies must be drawn up with refugees views and refugees empowerment as priority issues.

Conclusions and recommendations

This report has outlined some of the many issues faced by refugees (and asylum-seekers) in Europe – the reasons for their flight, the international legal conventions that determine their status, the national laws and institutions which govern their daily lives, and their prospects for the future. What the report cannot do is tell all the unique stories of the individual refugees – the tales of torture and persecution, the long wait for asylum and acceptance, the loneliness of exile, and, in a few cases, the triumph over adversity and the return to a liberated land.

In the mid-1990s, for the first time in recent years, the number of refugees arriving in many European countries has started to decline. This has occurred at a time when the number of refugees and internally displaced people worldwide is growing and there is no evidence to suggest that the factors which cause refugees to flee have decreased. It is therefore anticipated that the number of refugees and displaced people worldwide will continue to grow.

If these trends continue, there is a risk that states in the South will not be prepared to host refugee populations which are proportionately so much greater than those in Europe. If Europe labels refugees as 'burdensome', adopts measures to effectively prevent asylum-seekers from reaching European borders and refuses to grant asylum to those who manage to make a legitimate claim, then it is likely that other regions of the world may soon follow suit. Refugees in need of protection will be the casualties.

These recommendations fall into four categories; first, recommendations to prevent the root cause of refugee movements; second, recommendations to strengthen good practice and remedy weaknesses in governmental treatment of asylum-seekers and refugees; third, recommendations on the process of deciding policy on refugee issues; and finally, recommendations for good practice in the settlement and long-term development and integration of refugees in Europe.

The root causes of refugees

1   Governments should actively investigate connections between violations of human and minority rights, persecution, intolerance and harassment and subsequent displacement of populations. Where such links are found to exist, governments may wish to re-orientate their foreign policy to promote cooperation between communities and conflict prevention, and address the economic factors which can exacerbate tensions between communities.

2   The EU, Council of Europe, OECD and other European bodies should individually and jointly aim to meet the UN target of aid monies reaching 1 per cent of GDP. Development assistance and trade should be clearly linked to the active promotion and observance of minority and human rights.

3   Governments should recognize the direct links between the sales of arms to regimes violating minority and human rights, and consequent moral responsibilities towards individuals and groups who have sought international protection as a result of having been attacked, threatened, injured or tortured with such weapons.

Urgent concerns and immediate possibilities

4   There should be an active search for a coherent European refugee assistance system, which is just and consistent with international legal standards. As well as complying with provisions on the non-*refoulement* of refugees, states must also respect and not seek to impede the fundamental human right to seek asylum as set out in Article 14 of the Universal Declaration of Human Rights.

5   States should ratify and implement the 1990 Dublin Convention relating to responsibility for determination of asylum claims. Until that Convention is ratified and implemented states should suspend the removal of asylum-seekers to a 'safe third country'.

6   Refugees originating from any particular state should not be assumed to necessarily share a culture, language or viewpoint. Sensitivity to minorities within communities is essential to those involved with the settlement of refugee populations.

Longer term concerns

7   All those people claiming to be refugees should have their individual cases examined fairly, in a way consistent with the due process of law and with an opportunity for independent review or appeal.

8   Asylum-seekers should not be assumed to be, and treated, as 'immigrants in disguise'. Immigration control policies should never deny the right of an asylum-seeker to seek asylum from persecution.

9   Legal protection should be granted generously by European states to people who, although they may not

meet the criteria of the 1951 Convention and the 1967 Protocol, cannot safely return to their country of nationality or origin.

10 Asylum-seekers should not be treated as virtual criminals and should not be detained or subjected to unreasonable restrictions in their movements. The entire procedure from arrival of asylum-seekers to the final decision on their status should be as short as is consistent with following a full and fair process of law.

11 Asylum-seekers should be eligible for reasonable levels of financial support, accommodation and other material help while their claims are being considered, and while they exercise any right to an independent review of any decision not to grant asylum.

12 States should give serious consideration to the possibility of establishing an international court similar to the European Court of Human Rights which would be able to review the cases of individuals alleging that states had failed to comply with their obligations arising as signatories of the 1951 Convention and 1967 Protocol.

13 Governments in Europe cannot afford to ignore the indirect effects of their policies globally. There should be continued financial support by European governments for refugee programmes outside Europe. This financial support should not be seen as replacing the need for Europe to abide by its undertakings on refugees under international law.

14 Recognized refugees should be entitled to the same rights as nationals regarding economic, social and cultural rights such as: subsistence, housing, education, training and employment, language, and religious practice. This should include the same rights as any national to undertake political activities.

15 Refugees have special needs concerning their long-term development. Practical needs include language training, education programmes, and employment retraining. Their deeper cultural, personal needs should be respected through support for their own languages, culture and way of life, and for social, medical and psychological programmes geared to their needs. Special targeted programmes are essential. States should seek to implement the provisions of the Declaration on the Rights of Persons belonging to National or Ethnic Religious and Linguistic Minorities, and the Convention on the Rights of the Child and other relevant international instruments in setting up such provision.

16 Governments and NGOs should promote public education for the host population on the causes behind refugee flight, on the problems faced by refugees and on the contributions made by refugees. Racist and xenophobic expressions against refugees should be addressed under legal provisions as well as by advocacy campaigns on behalf of refugees.

NOTES

1 Marrus M.R., *The Unwanted: European Refugees in the Twentieth Century*, New York, OUP, 1985.

2 Hope-Simpson, J., *The Refugee Problem: Report of a Survey*, London, OUP, 1939, p. 230.

3 *Ibid.*, p. 4–5.

4 Coles, G.J.L., 'Solutions to the Problem of Refugees and the Protection of Refugees', a background study prepared for the Round Table on Durable Solutions and the Protection of Refugees, convened by the Office of the UNHCR in conjunction with the International Institute of Humanitarian Law, Geneva, 1989.

5 Gallagher, D., *The Era of Refugees: The Evolution of the International Refugee System*, Washington, Refugee Policy Group, 1989, p. 4.

6 Marrus, M.R., *Op. Cit.*, pp. 40–50; and Hope-Simpson, J., *Op. Cit.*, pp. 29–61. See MRG Reports, *The Armenians*, and *Minorities in the Balkans*, and Rapports du GDM, *Les Assyro Chaldéens: Un Peuple Oubli de l'Histoire*.

7 A wide variety of figures were cited and, as Hope-Simpson notes 'they were originally made at a time of obvious and ample room for error', *Op. Cit.*, p. 80.

8 Gallagher, D., *Op. Cit.*, p. 6.

9 Marrus, M.R., *Op. Cit.*; p. 86–7, Gallagher, D., *Ibid.*, p. 7.

10 *Ibid.*, p. 8.

11 Costa-Lascoux, J., 'Réfugiés et demandeurs d'asile en Europe', *Revue Européenne des Migrations Internationales*, vol. 3, nos 1–2, le 3e trimestre 1987, pp. 240–1.

12 Gallagher, D., *Op. Cit.*, p. 13.

13 Wasserstein, B., *Britain and the Jews of Europe*, Oxford, OUP, 1988, p. 8; Coles, G.J.L., *Op. Cit.*, p. 34.

14 Coles, G.J.L., *Ibid.*, p. 34.

15 Gallagher, D., *Op. Cit.*, p.15; Marrus, M.R., *Op. Cit.*, pp. 170–2; Coles, G.J.L., *Ibid.*, pp. 38–40.

16 Marrus, M.R., *Ibid.*, p. 178.

17 Proudfoot, M.J., *European Refugees: 1939–52*, London, Faber and Faber, 1957, p. 21.

18 Marrus, M.R., *Op. Cit.*, p. 330.

19 Gallagher, D., *Op. Cit.*, p. 24.

20 For example, *Le Monde*, 15 January 1988, reports the burning of 138,000 copies of the January issue of *Refugees*, the UNHCR magazine, on the order of Jean-Pierre Hocke, the then High Commissioner, and the protest that ensued. It was alleged that this decision was motivated by the desire not to offend the government of the Federal Republic of Germany whose policy on refugees was discussed in the issue. According to *The Guardian*, 1 August 1990, the US administration has warned the UNHCR that Washington might withdraw funds for certain refugee projects if UNHCR became involved with the British mandatory repatriation scheme of Vietnamese refugees from Hong Kong.

21 Melander, G., *The Two Refugee Definitions*, Lund, Raoul Wallenberg Institute, Report no. 4, 1987, pp. 9–22.

22 UNHCR, Geneva, 1979.

23 Factors influencing the interpretation of the Convention will be examined later in the report.

24 Casella. A, 'Asylum-seekers in Europe: a humanitarian quandary', *The World Today*, November 1988, pp. 187–91.

25 Signatories to the Convention only: Madagascar, Monaco, Mozambique. Signatories to the Protocol only: Swaziland, USA, Venezuela.

26 Austria, Belgium, Cyprus, Denmark, Finland, France, Germany, Greece, Iceland, Republic of Ireland, Italy, Liechtenstein, Luxembourg, Malta, Netherlands, Norway, Portugal, San Marino, Spain, Sweden, Switzerland, Turkey, UK.

27 Paludan, A., 'The new refugees in Europe', *Summary of the Report on Problems of Refugees and Exiles in Europe*, Geneva, International University Exchange Fund on behalf of the Working Group on Refugees and Exiles in Europe, 1974, pp. 3–47.

28 Zarjevski, M., *A Future Preserved: International Assistance to Refugees*, Oxford, Pergammon Press/UNHCR, 1988.

29 Forty-one African states are signatory to the OAU Convention.

30 Ecumenical Consultation on Asylum and Protection, *Mission Statement*, Zurich, 27 April – 2 May 1986.

31 Cels, J., *A Liberal and Humane Policy for Refugees and Asylum-seekers: Still a Realistic Policy Option?*, OUP, December 1986, p. 35.

32 Bettati, M., *L'Asile Politique en Question*, Paris, PUF, 1985.

33 Soulier, G., 'Droit d'asile et souverainet de l'état', in *Droit et Réfugiés*, Actes no. 40, pp. 19– 21, p. 20.

34 Belgium, Denmark, Germany, the Netherlands (B status is no longer granted in the Netherlands), Sweden and Switzerland have or have had these categories.

35 Council of Europe Parliamentary Assembly, *Report on the Situation of De Facto Refugees*, Doc. 3642, 5 August 1975, p. 11.

36 Hocke, J-P., 'Beyond humanitarianism: the need for political will to resolve today's refugee problem', Refugee Studies Programme, Joyce Pearce Memorial Lecture, Oxford University, 29 November 1986.

37 Kunz, E.F., 'The refugees in flight: kinetic models and forms of displacement', *International Migration Review*, vol. 7, no. 2, 1973, pp. 125–46.

38 Zolberg, A., et al., *Escape from Violence; Conflict and the Refugee Crisis in the Developing World*, Oxford, OUP, 1989, p. 68.

39 Hathaway, J.C., 'The evolution of refugee status in international law: 1920–50', *International and Comparative Law Quarterly*, no. 33, 1984.

40 *Ibid.*

41 ECRE, Temporary protection note from the Ad Hoc Meeting of ECRE agencies, Schipol, 12 February 1993.

42 *World Refugee Survey 1996*, Immigration Services of America, Washington DC.

43 Source of statistical data: *UNHCR by Numbers 1996*, UNHCR/PI/Numb-uk3.pm5/July 1996 (quoted by Türk, Conference on Refugee Rights and Realities University of Nottingham, 30 November 1996, Draft Paper, 'The Role of the United Nations High Commissioner for Refugees (UNHCR) in the Development of International Refugee Law').

44 Austria, Belgium, Denmark, Finland, France, Germány, Italy, Netherlands, Norway, Spain, Sweden, Switzerland, UK. Source: *IGC report 1996*, ECRE.

45 ECRE country report, October 1996.

46 Austria, Belgium, Denmark, Finland, France, Germany, Greece, Italy, Ireland, Netherlands, Norway, Portugal, Spain, Sweden, Switzerland, UK. Source: ECRE country reports, IGC, UNHCR. NB: figure not available for the number of asylum-seekers in Austria in 1995.

47 Source: *ECRE Annual Report 1994* and Eurostat.

48 Document HCR/1MFY/1992/2 of 24 July 1992, quoted in Appendix 5, *Report of ECRE Biannual General Meeting*, April 1993.

49 Survey of the implementation of temporary protection, UNHCR, Appendix 8, *Report of Biannual ECRE General Meeting, Ibid.*

50 Report on temporary protection in states in Europe, North America, and Australia, August 1995, Secretariat of the Inter-governmental Consultations on Asylum refugee and migration policies in Europe, North America and Australia.

51 ECRE Country Report, May 1996.

52 Figures for 1991 to 1994 taken from Report on temporary protection in states in Europe, North America, and Australia, *Ibid.* ECRE figure for 1995 taken from country reports, May 1996. *Op.Cit.*

53 ECRE country reports, May 1996 and October 1995

54 Survey on the implementation of temporary protection, Humanitarian Issues Working Group of the International Conference on the Former Yugoslavia, UNHCR, June 1994.

55 Survey of the implementation of temporary protection, *Op.Cit.*

56 Report on temporary protection in states in Europe, North America, and Australia, August 1995, *Op. Cit.*

57 ECRE country reports, May 1996

58 ECRE country reports, October 1995.

59 Report on temporary protection in states in Europe, North America, and Australia, August 1995, *Op.Cit.*

60 ECRE country reports, October 1995.

61 ECRE country reports, 1996.

62 Report on temporary protection in states in Europe, North America, and Australia, August 1995, *Op.Cit*

63 ECRE country reports, October 1995.

64 Report on temporary protection in states in Europe, North America, and Australia, August 1995, *Op.Cit.*

65 ECRE country reports, May 1996.

66 Report on temporary protection in states in Europe, North America, and Australia, August 1995. *Op.City.*

67 ECRE country report, May 1996.

68 ECRE country report, October 1994.

69 ECRE country report, October 1995.

70 Report on temporary protection in states in Europe, North America, and Australia, August 1995, *Op. Cit.*

71 *Asylum Statistics, United Kingdom 1995*, Home Office Statistical Bulletin, Government Statistical Service, May 1996.

72 As note 44, although Ireland is omitted. Source: UNHCR 1995.

73 Source: *Asylum Statistics United Kingdom 1995, Op.Cit.*

74 Source: ECRE country reports, October 1996.

75 ECRE, Participants' meeting, October 1988.

76 ECRE, *Towards Harmonisation of Refugee Policies in Europe? A Contribution to the Discussion*, London, ECRE, October 1988, p. 5.

77 Quoted in Rudge, P., 'The spirit: historical and social perspectives. The failure of the spirit', The Refugee Crisis, British and Canadian Responses, International Symposium, 4-7 January 1989, London, p. 4.

78 Soulier, G., 'Le respect du droit d'asile, peuve et garant du droit démocratique', *France Terre d'Asile: La Lettre d'Information*, no. 65, June 1987, pp. 8–18.

79 ECRE, Participants' meeting, October 1988.

80 ECRE European Lawyers Workshop on the Implementation of Article 1a of the Geneva Convention, Paris, 4–5 May 1985.

81 *Le Monde*, quoting Tiberghien, 19 April 1988.

82 *The Independent*, 22 February 1996.

83 Vetter, H.O., *Report on the Right of Asylum*, European Parliament, 23 February 1987, p. 9.

84 Submission by the Refugee Legal Centre of the Glidewell Panel, unpublished, March 1996, p. 3.

85 Vetter, H.O. *Op. Cit.*, p. 12.

86 Danish Refugee Council, *The Role of Airline Companies in the Asylum Procedure*, Copenhagen, 1988.

87 Submission by the Refugee Legal Centre to the Glidewell Panel, unpublished, March 1996, p. 39.

88 *France Terre d'Asile, La Lettre d'Information, Expulsions du 7 Décembre 1987 (Iranians, Turks et Kurdes de Turquie)*, Numéro spécial, March 1988.

89 Amnesty International, *Amnesty International's Concerns in Western Europe*, October 1986–March 1987, SF 87 10 110, EUR, 3 January 1987, April 1987.

90 ECRE, Participants' meeting, October 1988, p. 9.

91 ZDWF – Schriftenreihe Nr. 20 Elena/ZDWF: European Lawyers Workshop on Detention, Choice of Residence and Freedom of Movement of Asylum-seekers and Refugees, May 1987.

92 *Hansard*, 22 February 1994, col. 151.

93 Cohen, R., 'The detention of asylum-seekers in the UK' in D. Joly, and R. Cohen, (eds), *Reluctant Hosts: Europe and its Refugees*, Aldershot, Gower, 1987, pp. 145–62, p. 148.

94 ECRE, Participants' meeting, October 1988, p. 11.

95 For further information, see the *Survey on Legal and Social Conditions of Asylum Seekers and Refugees*, Danish Refugee Council, forthcoming, 1997.

96 ECRE, Participants' meeting, October 1988, p. 21.

97 Cels, J., *Op. Cit.*, p. 139.

98 ECRE, participants' meeting, April 1989.

99 Figures from the UK Home Office Immigration and General Unit, February 1996.

100 These are documented in detail in Joly, D., with Nettleton, C., and Poulton, H., *Refugees: Asylum in Europe?.*, London, MRG, 1992.

101 Council of Europe: Recommendation on the Harmonization of National Procedures relating to Asylum, Recommendation No. R(81)16.

102 This discussed refugees within the context of immigration and security and aimed to introduce a single visa area.

103 European Commission, *Avant-project de Proposition de Directive du Conseil Relative au Rapprochement des Règles Concernant le Droit d'Asile et le Status des Réfugiés*, June 1988, p. 31.

104 Schengen Agreement 1990, ch. 7, Art. 29–4.

105 *Ibid.*, ch. 6, Art. 26.

106 *Ibid.*, ch. 6, Art. 17–1,

107 Conseil, Communication à la Presse 09/10, 'Garanties minimales en matière de demandes d'asile', 1995

108 Schengen Agreement 1990, ch. 7, Art. 38.

109 *Ibid.*, ch. 4, Arts 21, 22.

110 Referred to as the Steering Group in the rest of the text.

111 European Council, Conclusions of the Presidency, European Council in Edinburgh, 1992.

112 Ad Hoc Group on Immigration, Brussels, 26 October 1992, SN 4282/92, WG1 1230. Proposal for the Asylum Sub-Group to the Ad Hoc Immigration Group, including Annex A, Draft report to Ministers from the Ad Hoc Group on Immigration.

113 For more detailed information, See Joly, D., 'The porous dam', *International Journal of Refugee Law*, vol. 6, pp. 159–94, 1994.

114 Ad Hoc Group on Immigration, Brussels, 16 November 1992, SN 4678/92, WG1 1266. Draft recommendation regarding practices followed by Member States on expulsion.

115 Ad Hoc Group on Immigration, Brussels, 25 May 1993, SN 3017/93, WG1 1516. Draft recommendation concerning checks on and expulsion of third country nationals residing or working without authorization.

116 Brochman, G., 'Immigration control, the welfare state and xenophobia towards an integrated Europe', *Migration*, no. 18, 1993, pp. 5–25.

117 Conseil, Communication à la presse, *Op.Cit.*

118 ECRE and Amnesty International, Press Release, 'ECRE and Amnesty International believe new EU minimum guarantees for asylum procedures are insufficient', 10 March 1995.

119 These are people who find themselves outside their country of origin when circumstances in that country change and who may be threatened with persecution were they to return.

120 UNHCR, 'Agents of persecution', note of March 1995.

121 ECRE, 'Note from the European Council on Refugees and Exiles on the harmonization of the interpretation of Article 1 of the 1951 Geneva Convention', and Standing Committee of experts in international immigration, refugee and criminal law, 'Who is a "refugee"?', Utrecht, June 1994.

122 ECRE, 'Note from the European Council on Refugees and Exiles', *Ibid.*

123 UNHCR, Information note on Article 1 of the 1951 Convention, 1995.

124 Ministers responsible for immigration, *Report to the European Council in Maastricht on Immigration and Asylum Policy*, Brussels, 3 December 1991, Annex 2.

125 Commission of the European Community, 'Communication from the Commission to the Council and the European Parliament on Immigration and Immigration and Asylum Policies', Com (94), Brussels, 23 February 1994.

126 Suhrke, A., 'Safeguarding the right to asylum', International Conference on Population and Development 1994, Expert Group Meeting on Population Distribution and Migration, Santa Cruz, Bolvia, 18–22 January 1993.

127 Secretariat of the Inter-governmental Consultations on Asylum, Refugee and Migration Policies in Europe, North America and Australia, Working Paper on Reception in the Region of Origin, September 1994.

128 ECRE, Temporary protection note from the Ad Hoc Meeting of ECRE agencies, *Op. Cit.*

129 UNHCR, 'Comprehensive response to the humanitarian crises in former Yugoslavia', Informal meeting on temporary protection, Geneva, 21 January 1993, Background note, p. 6.

130 UNHCR, 'Comprehensive response to the humanitarian crisis in former Yugoslavia'. Informal meeting on temporary protection, Geneva, 25 March 1993, Background note, Addendum, p. 2.

131 Kjaerum, M., 'Note on temporary protection in Europe in the '90s', for the CSCE Expert Seminar on Migration including Refugees and Displaced Persons, 20–24 April 1993, Warsaw.

132 Commission of the European Community, *Op. Cit.*

133 UNHCR, 'Comprehensive response to the humanitarian crisis in former Yugoslavia', 24 March 1993, *Op. Cit.*

134 UNHCR, 'Comprehensive response to the humanitarian crisis in former Yugoslavia', 21 January 1993, *Op. Cit.*

135 ECRE, 'Temporary protection note', *Op. Cit.*

136 HCR, 'Position du HCR sur la question de l'application de la Convention de Genève aux demandeurs d'asile en provenance de l'ex Yugoslavie', Paris, 2 December 1992.

137 *Migration News Sheet*, November 1995, no. 152/95–11.

138 Hathaway, J., et al, 'Towards the reformulation of international law', for discussion at consultative workshops in London and Washington, 4 and 11 October 1996.

139 Rudge, P., 'Rights of persons and temporary protection', The Committee on Migration Refugees and Demography, Parliamentary Assembly, Council of Europe, Paris, 12 April 1996.

140 Secretariat of the Inter-governmental Consultations on Asylum, 1995.

141 Goodwin-Gill, G., 'Refugee identity and the fading prospect of international protection', Nottingham, Conference on Refugee Rights and Realities, 30 November 1996.

142 Joly, D., 'The new asylum regime and temporary protection', Conference on Refugee Rights and Realities, 30 November 1996.

143 Joly, D. 'Temporary protection: the cornerstone of a new asylum regime', forthcoming.

144 Rudge, P., 'Rights of persons under temporary protection', *Op. Cit.*

145 Conditions of reception and settlement are continuously being downgraded. For further and more up to date information on these questions, see the forthcoming *Survey on Legal and Social Conditions of Asylum Seekers and Refugees*, *Op. Cit.*

146 *Collection of International Instruments Concerning Refugees*, Geneva, UNHCR, 1979, p. 102.

147 Council of Europe, Parliamentary Assembly, *Report on Living and Working Conditions of Refugees and Asylum-seekers*. Rapporteur Mr Boh, 26 March 1985.

148 EU Council, Note from the Presidency to the asylum group, 22 February 1996.

149 Joly D., 'Britain and its refugees: the case of the Chileans', *Migration 1987*, Band 1, Heft 1, pp. 91–108, p. 97.

150 Phillips, A.,'Employment as a key to settlement' in D.

Joly, and R. Cohen, *Op. Cit.* pp. 133–45, p. 136.

151 Lexa, F., 'Les réfugiés aujourd'hui', *Vie Sociale*, no. 1, Janvier 1985, pp. 3–9, p. 8.

152 Paludan, A., *Op. Cit.*, pp. 3–47, p. 27.

153 Joly, D., *Refugees from Vietnam in Birmingham: Community, Voluntary Agency and the Role of Local Authority*, Research paper, no. 9, CRER, 1988.

154 Council of Europe, Comité Européen sur les Migrations (CDMG), *Echanges de Vues Concernant la Condition Sociale des Réfugiés*, Strasbourg, 17 March 1988.

155 Council of Europe, Standing Conference of Local and Regional Authorities of Europe, 19th Session (Strasbourg 16–18 October 1984), Opinion No. 25 (1984) (1) on reception of refugees and asylum-seekers by local authorities.

156 UNHCR, *Social Services Workshop, Europe*, Geneva, 18–21 June 1984, p. 4.

157 Council of Europe, *Op. Cit.*

158 UNHCR, *The Integration of Refugees in Europe*, 1983, pp. 14–8; Council of Europe, Parliamentary Assembly, *Report on Living and Working Conditions of Refugees and Asylum- seekers*, (1), 26 March 1985, p. 6.

159 Centre for Employment Initiatives, *A Report on the Employment Situation of Refugees*, prepared for the UNHCR, London, CEI, 1984, p. 3.

160 UNHCR, Follow-up to the 1983 Seminar on the Integration of Refugees in Europe, *Report on the Second Meeting of the Contact Group (Geneva 6/11/84)*, 21 January 1985, p. 4.

161 Jones, P., *Vietnamese Refugees, A Study of their Reception and Resettlement in the United Kingdom*, Research and Planning Visit Paper 13, London, Home Office, 1982, p. 16.

162 Santa Cruz, M.J., 'Refugees from South East Asia in Spain: the challenge of hope' in D. Joly, and R. Cohen, *Op. Cit.* pp. 54–66.

163 Sayers, R., 'Resettling refugees: the Dutch model' in D. Joly, and R. Cohen, *Ibid*, pp. 19–39.

164 Council of Europe, Comité Europeén sur les Migration (CDMG), *Echange de vues Concernant la Condition Sociale des Réfugiés*, Note etablie par la Belgique, Strasbourg, 17 March 1988.

165 Joly, D., *Refugees from Vietnam in Birmingham, Op. Cit.*

166 Joly, D., 'The new asylum regime and temporary protection', *Op. Cit.*

167 Lohrmann, R., 'Un rapport du Conseil de l'Europe sur les mesures sociales prise par les pays membres en faveur des réfugiés politiques', *Hommes et Migrations*, no. 1010, 15 March 1981, 32e année, pp. 3–38.

168 'Une formation d'adaptation pour des assistants sociaux latino-américains', *Migrant Formation*, no. 41–2, October 1980, pp. 77–8.

169 Phillips, A., 'Employment as a key to settlement', *Op. Cit.*

170 'Pour l'insertion des réfugiés: création d'une entreprise Troyes', *France Terre d'Asile, La Lettre d'Information*, lettre no. 64, Mars 1987, pp. 19–25.

171 Centre for Employment Initiatives, *Op. Cit.*, p. 43.

172 Cruz Jordana, M. and Sanchez Pardo, L., 'Spanish resettlement programmes' in D. Joly, and R. Cohen, *Op. Cit.*, pp. 176–83.

173 Centre for Employment Initiatives, *Op. Cit.*

174 Vasquez, A., 'La scolarisation des adolescents latino-americains exilés', *Migrants Formation*, nos 41–2, October 1980, pp. 104–7.

175 Lohrmann, R., *Op. Cit.*, pp. 3–38.

176 Cimade-Information No. 11–12, 11 December 1983.

177 SSAE, *La Formation des Réfugiés*, Paris, SSAE, Décembre 1986.

178 Lohrmann, R., *Op. Cit.*, pp. 3–38.

179 Council of Europe, SCLRAE, 19th Session (Strasbourg 16–18 October 1984), Opinion No. 25 (1984) (1) on reception of refugees and asylum-seekers by local authorities, p. 2.

180 Field, S., *Op. Cit.*

181 *Ibid.*, pp. 48–9.

182 UNHCR, *Op. Cit.*, p. 4.

183 Council of Europe, *Op. Cit.*, p. 3.

184 UNHCR, *Op. Cit.*

185 Joint Working Group for Refugees from Chile in Britain, *Refugees from Chile: An Interim Report*, London, JWGR, 1975.

186 UNHCR, *Op. Cit.*, p. 16.

187 *The Times*, 13 February 1987.

188 *The Times*, 7 July 1987.

189 *The Guardian*, 17 March 1987.

190 ECRE, *Op. Cit*

191 International Social Services, Unaccompanied Minor Refugees in European Resettlement Countries, Seminar held by ISS, German Branch and ECRE, 13–16 March 1984, Frankfurt am Main.

BIBLIOGRAPHY

Bohm, *Report on Living and Working Conditions of Refugees and Asylum-Seekers*, Council of Europe Parliamentary Assembly, Doc 5380 revised, 26 March 1985.

Commission of the European Communities, *Communication from the Commission to the Council and the European Parliament on Immigration and Asylum Policies*, Com (94), Brussels, 23 February 1994.

Danish Refugee Council, *Survey on Legal and Social Conditions of Asylum Seekers and Refugees*, forthcoming, 1997.

Drücke, L., *Asylum Policies in a European Community without Internal Borders*, Churches Committee for Migrants in Europe, Briefing paper no. 9, October 1992.

ECRE, *Asylum in Europe: An Introduction, Volume 1*, London, ECRE, April 1993.

Gold, S.J., *Refugee Communities*, Newbury Park, Sage, 1992.

Goodwin-Gill, G., *The Refugee in International Law*, Oxford, Clarendon Press, 1983.

Hathaway, J.C., 'The evolution of refugee status in international law: 1920–1950, *International and Comparative Law Quarterly*, no. 33, 1984.

Hope-Simpson, J., *The Refugee Problem: Report of a Survey*, London, OUP, 1939.

Jaeger, G., 'Refugees in and from Central and Eastern Europe', *Oikoumene – Refugees* special issue, August 1991.

Joly, D., *Haven or Hell? Asylum Policies and Refugees in Europe*, Basingstoke, Macmillan, 1996.

Joly, D., with Cohen, R., (eds), *Reluctant Hosts: Europe and its Refugees*, Aldershot, Gower Press, 1989.

Joly, D., with Nettleton, C., Poulton, H., *Refugees: Asylum in Europe*, London, MRG, 1992.

Kay, D., *Chileans in Exile: Private Struggles, Public Lives*, London, Macmillan, 1987.

Kjaerum, M., *Note on Temporary Protection in Europe in the '90s for the CSCE Expert Seminar on Migration including Refugees and Displaced Persons*, Warsaw, April 1993.

Kunz, E., 'Exile and resettlement: refugee theory', *International Migration Review*, vol. 7, no. 2, 1981.

Marrus, M.R., *The Unwanted: European Refugees in the Twentieth Century*, New York, OUP, 1985.

Richmond, A.H., 'Sociological theories of international migration: the case of refugees', *Current Sociology*, 36: 2, 1988.

Rudge, P., *Fortress Europe in World Refugee Survey (1986 in Review)*, US Committee for Refugees, Washington, Virginia Hamilton, 1987.

UNHCR, *State of the World's Refugees: In Search of Solutions*, UNHCR, 1995.

Zolberg, A.R.; Suhrke, A.; Aguayo, S.; *Escape from Violence, Conflict and the Refugee Crisis in the Developing World*, Oxford, OUP, 1989.

About Minority Rights Group Reports

Minority Rights Group began publishing in 1970. Over two decades and 90 titles later, MRG's series of Reports are widely recognized internationally as authoritative, accurate and objective documents on the rights of minorities worldwide.

Over the years, subscribers to the series have received a wealth of unique material on ethnic, religious, linguistic and social minorities. The Reports are seen as an important reference by researchers, students, and campaigners and provide readers all over the world with valuable background data on many current affairs issues.

Six Reports are published every year. Each title, expertly researched and written, is approximately 32 pages and 20,000 words long and covers a specific minority issue.

Recent titles in our Report series include:

Africa	**Europe**
Burundi	Northern Ireland
Sudan	North Caucasus
Americas	**Middle East**
Maya of Guatemala	Beduin of the Negev
The Inuit of Canada	The Kurds
Afro-Central Americans	
Asia	**General**
Cambodia	Education Rights
Sri Lanka	Land Rights
Tajikstan	

If you have found this Report informative and stimulating, and would like to learn more about minority issues, please do subscribe to our report series. It is only with the help of our supporters that we are able to pursue our aims and objectives – to secure justice for disadvantaged groups around the world.

We currently offer a reduced annual rate for individual subscribers – please ring our Subscription Desk on **+44 (0)171 978 9498** for details. Payment can be easily made by MasterCard or Visa over the telephone or by post.

All enquiries to: *Sales Department*
Minority Rights Group
379 Brixton Road
London SW9 7DE
UK

Fax: +44 (0)171 738 6265
E mail: minority rights@mrg.sprint.com